What People Are Saying About
Chicken Soup for the NASCAR® Soul . . .

"*Chicken Soup for the NASCAR Soul* not only takes you inside the tracks, the cars and the garages of the sport's biggest personalities, but it also takes you inside their hearts and minds."

Jeff Gordon

"Racing around a track at almost 200 miles per hour is hard. Racing through life at even greater speeds is even harder. *Chicken Soup for the NASCAR Soul* will help to make your ride more enjoyable."

Bobby Labonte

"Not only is NASCAR great fun, it is a sport full of some of the most classic personalities and events you will find anywhere. *Chicken Soup for the NASCAR Soul* celebrates the sport's great history and the characters that made NASCAR."

Robby Gordon

"*Chicken Soup for the NASCAR Soul* is more than high speed and horsepower. It shows off the heart and humanity of those involved in the sport so many Americans love."

Mike Smith
director of public relations
Martinsville Speedway

"Racing is about more than just pure speed. It is also about conviction, dedication, faith, trust, courage and an unyielding drive to be your best. *Chicken Soup for the NASCAR Soul* captures all of this in these wonderful stories of insight and inspiration."

Ned Jarrett

"I can't win a race without the help of my entire team. *Chicken Soup for the NASCAR Soul* helps us realize that we need the same team approach to winning at life."

Michael Waltrip

"Just as the names Andretti, Petty and Foyt mean motorsports, so too the name of *Chicken Soup for the Soul* means great stories of hope and inspiration. *Chicken Soup for the NASCAR Soul* is perfect in keeping with that great tradition."

John Andretti

"*Chicken Soup for the NASCAR Soul* is a pure winner."

Ricky Rudd

"NASCAR provides excitement to all its fans through side-by-side racing. *Chicken Soup for the NASCAR Soul* brings you side-by-side with your favorite NASCAR personality with real stories about life in the racing community."

Max Helton
founder, Motor Racing Outreach and
International Motorsport Services

CHICKEN SOUP
FOR THE
NASCAR® SOUL

Inspirational Stories of Courage, Speed and Overcoming Adversity

Jack Canfield
Mark Victor Hansen
Matthew E. Adams
Jeff Aubery
Kirk Autio

Health Communications, Inc.
Deerfield Beach, Florida

www.bcibooks.com
www.chickensoupforthesoul.com

We would like to acknowledge the many publishers and individuals who granted us permission to reprint the cited material. (Note: The stories that were penned anonymously, that are in the public domain or that were written by Jack Canfield, Mark Victor Hansen, Matthew E. Adams, Jeff Aubery or Kirk Autio are not included in this listing.)

All photographs in this book (with the exception of the photo on page 258) have been reprinted with the permission of NASCAR, Inc. Copyright 2003 National Association for Stock Car Auto Racing, Inc.

The Little Girl's Shoe, It's Not All About Sunday and *Simple Pleasures.* Reprinted by permission of Carol Einarsson. ©2001 Carol Einarsson.

Roush's Angel Always on Duty. Copyright 2002, USA TODAY. Reprinted with permission.

One Last Time Around. Reprinted by permission of Dennis Yohnka. ©2002 Dennis Yohnka.

(Continued on page 267)

Library of Congress Cataloging-in-Publication Data

Chicken soup for the NASCAR soul : inspirational stories of courage, speed, and
  overcoming adversity / [edited by] Jack Canfield . . . [et al.].
    p. cm.
  ISBN 0-7573-0100-2 (trade paper)
    1. Stock car racing—United States—Miscellanea. 2. Automobile racing
  drivers—United States—Conduct of life. 3. NASCAR (Association) I. Canfield,
  Jack, date.

  GV1029.9.S74C45 2003
  796.72'0973—dc21

                                        2003041695

© 2003 Jack Canfield and Mark Victor Hansen
ISBN 0-7573-0100-2 (trade paper)

Publisher: Health Communications, Inc.
           3201 S.W. 15th Street
           Deerfield Beach, FL 33442-8190

Cover design by Lisa Camp
Inside formatting by Lawna Patterson Oldfield

We dedicate this book to the fans
of NASCAR. Your passion
and spirit for the sport
keep NASCAR and all its
history alive for generations to come.

Contents

2. UP TO SPEED

3. THE WORLD'S GREATEST FANS

4. FROM THE HEART

Acknowledgments

The path to *Chicken Soup for the NASCAR Soul* has been made all the more beautiful by the many companions who have been there with us along the way. Our heartfelt gratitude to:

Our families, who have been chicken soup for our souls!

Inga, Travis, Riley, Christopher, Oran and Kyle, for all their love and support.

Patty, Elisabeth and Melanie Hansen, for once again sharing and lovingly supporting us in creating yet another book.

Donna, Austin and C. J. Adams; Patty, J. T. and Chandler Aubery; Nancy and Molly Autio. Your love and support have allowed us the time and space to create a wonderful book.

Our publisher, Peter Vegso, for his vision and commitment to bringing *Chicken Soup for the Soul* to the world.

Patty Aubery, for being there on every step of the journey, with love, laughter and endless creativity.

Heather McNamara and D'ette Corona, for producing our final manuscript with magnificent ease, finesse and care. Thanks for making the final stages of production such a breeze!

Leslie Riskin, for her care and loving determination to secure our permissions and get everything just right.

Nancy Autio and Barbara LoMonaco, for nourishing us with truly wonderful stories and cartoons.

Dana Drobny and Kathy Brennan-Thompson, for listening and being there throughout with humor and grace.

Maria Nickless, for her enthusiastic marketing and public-relations support and a brilliant sense of direction.

Patty Hansen, for her thorough and competent handling of the legal and licensing aspects of the *Chicken Soup for the Soul* books. You are magnificent at the challenge!

Laurie Hartman, for being a precious guardian of the *Chicken Soup* brand.

Veronica Romero, Teresa Esparza, Robin Yerian, Stephanie Thatcher, Jody Emme, Trudy Marschall, Michelle Adams, Dee Dee Romanello, Shanna Vieyra, Lisa Williams, Gina Romanello, Brittany Shaw, Dena Jacobson, Tanya Jones, Mary McKay and David Coleman, who support Jack's and Mark's businesses with skill and love.

Christine Belleris, Allison Janse, Lisa Drucker and Susan Tobias, our editors at Health Communications, Inc., and Kathy Grant, editorial assistant, for their devotion to excellence.

Terry Burke, Tom Sand, Lori Golden, Kelly Johnson Maragni, Randee Feldman, Patricia McConnell, Kim Weiss, Paola Fernandez-Rana, Teri Peluso, and the marketing, sales, public-relations and administration departments at Health Communications, Inc., for doing such an incredible job supporting our books.

Tom Sand, Claude Choquette and Luc Jutras, who manage year after year to get our books translated into thirty-six languages around the world.

The art department at Health Communications, Inc., for their talent, creativity and unrelenting patience in producing book covers and inside designs that capture the essence of *Chicken Soup:* Larissa Hise Henoch, Lawna Patterson Oldfield, Andrea Perrine Brower, Lisa Camp, Anthony Clausi and Dawn Von Strolley Grove.

Thank you to Paul Krupin for his help in soliciting for truly wonderful stories.

Thank you to Jennifer White at NASCAR, Tom Archer at ESPN, Dr. Jerry Punch at ABC/ESPN, Tim Sullivan, Tony Ragano, Fran Gollow and Tony Marderosian for their friendship and support in making this book a reality.

Thank you to Sherryl and Stan Creekmore at Signature Racing for supplying us with wonderful photos.

And to our glorious panel of readers who helped us make the final selections and made invaluable suggestions on how to improve the book: Donna Adams, Richard Bacon, Tom Betts, Bill Creamer, Dominic and Jennifer Dale, Mark Dennen, Joshua Hrehovcik, Carl Johnson, Heidi Johnson, LeAnn Krieg, Frank Lomonaco, Gregory Nelson, Thomas Pickett, Wayne Spodnick, Todd Stoeffler, Denene Van Hecker, John Weber, and most of all, everyone who submitted their heartfelt stories, poems, quotes and cartoons for possible inclusion in this book. While we were not able to use everything you sent, we know that each word came from a magical place flourishing within your soul. May the spirit of nature carry you gently toward peace!

Because of the size of this project, we may have left out the names of some people who contributed along the way. If so, we are sorry, but please know that we really do appreciate you very much.

We are truly grateful and love you all!

Introduction

NASCAR has always been a reflection of life. From its parochial southern roots to its immensely successful explosion onto the national scene, it is full of speed, courage, power, bravery and wholesome family values that combine to make the sport a uniquely American experience.

Who cannot relate to racing through life only inches from your competition and an unforgiving wall while traveling at speeds close to two hundred miles per hour? Don't we all need to know that we have a support crew of our own to help fine-tune and prepare us for our own daily race through life?

Chicken Soup for the NASCAR Soul perfectly captures the metaphor of racing as life in these wonderful and inspiring stories of overcoming adversity and the need for family and friends to help you overcome life's challenges. If ever we desire to feel a sense of community, all we need to do is go to a NASCAR race. The experience is so compelling and so much fun that any newcomer is instantly hooked. There is no other experience in the world of sports that combines such a mass celebration of fanaticism as the backdrop for an intense athletic competition. Your body will shudder with the screams of 250,000 of your impassioned fellow fans while the deafening roar of the cars form a blinding parade of power and spectacle.

Within the pages of this book, you will find humorous stories that illustrate the down-home and unique "NASCAR personalities," both past and present, who helped frame the sport as we know it. You will enjoy stories that are intended to make you laugh, think and, in some cases, gain a new perspective. This book is also full of stories from the sport's devoted fans who share with us how NASCAR has touched their lives. Perhaps the most emotional stories are those about the heroes who are no longer with us, including the sport's icon, Dale Earnhardt, who is featured in a special tribute chapter.

We compiled *Chicken Soup for the NASCAR Soul* in the hope of capturing the mystery and wonder of this sport with stories that will inspire you, provide you with insight and leave you with a whole new appreciation for NASCAR.

Share with Us

We would love to hear your reactions to the stories in this book. Please let us know what your favorite stories were and how they affected you.

We also invite you to send us stories you would like to see published in future editions of *Chicken Soup for the Soul*. Please send submissions to:

Chicken Soup for the Soul
P.O. Box 30880
Santa Barbara, CA 93130
fax: 805-563-2945

You can also visit or access e-mail at the *Chicken Soup for the Soul* site:

www.chickensoupforthesoul.com

We hope you enjoy reading this book as much as we enjoyed compiling, editing and writing it.

1

THE SPIRIT
OF NASCAR®

*The people who get on in this world are
the people who get up and look for the
circumstances they want, and if they
can't find them, make them.*

Brett Bodine

The Little Girl's Shoe

Racing is supposed to be dangerous. It always has been dangerous and hopefully always will be dangerous. If it were not dangerous and did not require a certain level of skill, then everybody interested would do it, and there would be nobody left to fill the grandstands.

Neil Bonnett

In any given generation, there seems to be a day that everyone remembers. My parents remember exactly where they were when President Kennedy was killed. The next generation remembers where they were when they heard about John Lennon. Race fans, however, remember exactly where they were whenever they heard news that made us all a little less innocent about racing.

For me, the first time was Davey Allison. It wasn't Walter Cronkite, but rather ESPN reporter Charlie Steiner who broke the news. When Charlie broke in, it was never good news. Charlie always seemed like a nice guy, but despite that, he was never a welcome face on my television during the day. You see, Charlie broke into programming one day and told me that Davey Allison had died after suffering closed-head injuries and brain swelling resulting from a helicopter crash. It seemed as if history was repeating itself when Charlie broke in one day the following year and told me about Ernie Irvan's crash.

But Ernie was different. He was the one who took over Davey's car, even when many thought he wasn't worthy. He had a certain nickname, Swervin' Irvan, and some weren't too quick to forget it. Yet he seemed to dress himself in Davey's old car in a way that made him better. When he won his first race with his new team, he tore open his uniform to reveal he'd been wearing a Davey Allison shirt underneath. He became the adopted son of the entire state of Alabama.

And then he crashed—170 miles per hour into a concrete wall. There was Charlie reporting on Ernie's injuries, which sounded eerily similar to those Davey had suffered. In a wreck at Michigan, he'd suffered a closed-head injury and brain swelling; he was unconscious and not expected to live through the night. Every race fan knows what to look for when a car is seen after a wreck. A tarp means there has been a fatality, and they need to preserve the car for investigation. When Charlie showed me Ernie's car, it was covered with a tarp.

Ernie had a 10 percent chance of survival, which everyone knows means he's going to die, but no doctor is brave enough to admit it. The hospital set up special phone lines to accommodate the barrage of phone calls checking on Ernie. They updated the phone messages two or three times a day, and devoted fans called at least that many times. I was no different and, day after day, I waited for news, expecting the worst, but always praying for the best.

Ernie's devoted wife, Kim, sat at his bedside hour after hour. The first day she had placed a shoe in Ernie's hand and closed his fingers around it. It wasn't just any shoe; it was the baby shoe of his tiny daughter, Jordan. When Ernie's fingers were closed around it, Kim and the doctors were unable to get him to release his grip. Unconscious, expected to die, and yet there was Ernie, grasping to life and the family that he wasn't ready to leave.

Miraculously, news came weeks later that Ernie was waking up. It was believed that while he managed to survive, he certainly wouldn't race again. Racing is one step short of a disease, though, and Ernie wasn't ready to live his life without it. He believed he would come back to race again, and in just over a year, doctors and NASCAR cleared him to drive.

Some time later, every fan who had sent a card to Ernie received a card in return. Ernie had written to us all expressing his thanks for our support and prayers. He wrote, "My thanks to the good Lord for answering the prayers of all my family, friends and fans as well as the entire racing fraternity, thereby granting me another chance at life. Life is a beautiful gift God has given to each and every one of us. Take time each day to give him praise and thank him for all your blessings, for they can be taken away without warning."

Though some doubted if he still had the sharpness of skills required to run in the top level of stock-car racing, Ernie persisted. His comeback was complete when Ernie returned to Michigan, the track that tried to stop him, and *won* less than three years after his accident. There wasn't a dry eye in the house.

Ernie has since retired from racing, but his courage and determination will always inspire race fans and others. The next time you're feeling discouraged or defeated, remember the man, holding onto a little girl's shoe, unwilling to give up. It's no wonder Ernie was selected to carry the Olympic Torch during its journey from Atlanta to Salt Lake City. He *is* a hero.

Carol Einarsson

Roush's Angel Always on Duty

The wealthy, thrill-seeking NASCAR team owner shouldn't be alive. But he is, his life spared by a humble man who, among other things, was trained to kill. Until their unexpected, harrowing meeting in a cold Alabama lake eighteen days ago, Larry Hicks had never heard of Jack Roush. Now they can never be separated.

"He and I will forever be joined by this. I never will forget or get past the fact that he saved my life," Roush said Sunday from an Ann Arbor, Michigan, hospital.

Goodness knows, Hicks didn't have to dive into danger last month. The retired fifty-two-year-old Marine had a wife, children and grandchildren to consider. He was fighting cancer and the effects of chemotherapy and radiation. He was completing his master's degree so he could teach. Roush was the inveterate risk taker, Hicks a homebody.

"Up until this time, the most excitement I had was two grandchildren in the room at the same time," Hicks said during the weekend at Richmond International Raceway, site of Sunday's NASCAR Winston Cup race. He was invited by the Marine Corps, which sponsors a NASCAR Busch Series car.

He wasn't looking to become a hero. He already had

done admirable public service for two decades, including a tour of Vietnam. As a sergeant major, he was given a medical discharge in 1990 about the time his infantry unit was dispatched to Kuwait. "It was kind of heartbreaking I couldn't go with them," he said. "But had things not happened that way, Mr. Roush wouldn't be alive right now."

During that early April evening, Hicks was faced with pulling a faceless, nameless pilot from a submerged airplane cockpit, even as high-octane fuel swirled in the water near a smoking engine.

It's tempting to say he had a decision to make. But, really, he didn't. With bad knees and bad lungs, Larry Hicks sprinted to that lake.

"You have to understand, in the Marine Corps they talk about doing the right thing when it has to be done. To me, that was the right thing to do," said Hicks, who suffered fuel vapor burns to his trachea, bronchial tubes, arms and chest. "I don't know of a single Marine who would not have tried to do that. That's why I have a real problem with the hero part, because I didn't do anything other than what the Marine Corps trained me to do."

Hicks and his wife, Donna, were in their Troy, Alabama, home preparing to watch the news when she noticed a small red aircraft overhead.

"Look at that plane. Isn't it pretty?" she said.

Roush, flying solo in an unfamiliar aircraft and celebrating his sixtieth birthday, has no recollection to this day of what happened. The twin-engine, ultralight plane ran into a power line, flipped and plunged into about eight feet of water.

Hicks turned back and looked at Donna. "Whatever happens," he said, "I love you."

While she called 911, her husband quickly maneuvered a fourteen-foot johnboat to the crash site. Utilizing training designed to free military pilots trapped under water, he began a series of dives. The first time, nothing. The second time, he brushed Roush's head. On his third attempt, he was able to grab Roush, who was unconscious. He had compound fractures of his left leg, broken ribs, a punctured lung and massive head trauma. A trickle of blood flowed from his mouth. "He was not breathing—he had drowned," Hicks said.

He released Roush from his seat, pushed off the bottom and brought him to the surface, where he used his own body to prop up Roush in the water. During a modified Heimlich maneuver, water poured from Roush's mouth. Hicks began to administer CPR and, with his fifth breath of life, Roush began breathing. Soon, emergency personnel arrived and placed Roush in an ambulance. When Hicks was told whose life he had saved, he replied, "Okay, guys, but I still don't know who you are talking about."

They were formally introduced a week later at a Birmingham hospital. For a while, no one uttered a word. Then they hugged and cried until there wasn't a dry eye in the room. "You have to understand," Hicks said. "Having been in the Marine Corps, you don't really express your emotions that well."

There are NASCAR heroes. And there are real-life heroes. Larry Hicks is both.

Jon Saraceno

One Last Time Around

Dream big. There is little power in little plans.

H. Jackson Brown Jr.

On warm Friday nights in the summer of 1963, fans at the little Sugar Island Speedway, outside of Aroma Park, Illinois, cheered for an "older" driver in a lilac purple 1957 Chevy with a red #4 on the door.

Joe Weaver was at the wheel, wearing white pants and a white shirt, black engineer boots and a helmet that looked more like today's bicycle headgear. He wasn't a romanticized version of a dirt-track driver. He was well beyond the twenty-something looks of a James Dean–style daredevil.

Still, he was the reigning king of the power slide, and he made dozens of laps each summer with a smile on his face and the checkered flag in his hand.

Time had begun to erode his skills later in that decade, and then a highway accident sent him into a long, painful rehabilitation period. He never raced again. Instead, his focus for the next two years would be to simply survive.

By the year 2000, Joe was in a local nursing home. He regained some abilities, but was never the same after the accident. He was confined to a wheelchair now that severe arthritis multiplied the discomfort in those joints so damaged in that wreck.

The staff at the home had heard all about the stories of his racing days, but it wasn't until administrators initiated a special one-more-wish program that they were able to put that information to use. Prior to Joe's wish, they had arranged simple requests such as a romantic Valentine's Day dinner for a couple, a visit to a nearby farm for one lady and other activities that turned back the clock in special ways for the residents.

For the old man in Room 325, the wish-fulfillment plan would require more extensive efforts—he wanted to be in his stock car again. Would the local track cooperate? Could they find a car like Joe used to drive? Could they even hope to pry his stiff, achy body into a stock car with the doors welded shut?

Jim O'Connor, a man who once shared the quarter-mile oval with Joe, now managed the local track, the Kankakee Motor Speedway. He quickly approved the idea and set about finding a 1957 Chevy that might still be racing. He discovered one in the Street Stock Division of a track nearly one hundred miles to the south. The car owner/driver, Leroy Nelson, easily agreed to the plan, and he began installing a passenger seat for Joe.

The night for the wish come true arrived with a threat of rain. The temperatures were cool, but the nursing-home staff bundled up their celebrity (plus a dozen other residents who wanted to see Joe's special moment). Of course, Joe's family and scores of friends turned out, too.

Wrapped in a blanket in his wheelchair, the weak-looking former driver appeared a bit lost, not too sure of the faces when former fans and competitors introduced themselves. He seemed to focus only on the moment when he would return to the track.

It began to sprinkle, and time trials were interrupted to wait out the showers. Joe was taken to a pavilion out of the rain. While he was surrounded by well-wishers, his mood was obviously dampened by the apparent loss of his chance to relive a little of his glory days.

At some point (no one knows who made the decision), it was concluded that it was now or never. The car was brought up as close as possible to the pit gate. Joe was wheeled over, and the ordeal of getting him into the car began. Using the blanket to cautiously move him, Joe was lifted through the back window and slid into the seat by a team of family members, drivers and nursing-home staff members.

He moaned in pain, but told them to continue. He was buckled in with the bulky blanket around him. The fans, nearly two thousand that night, stayed for this moment—despite the cold and the fact that this program was going to be rained out. And they stood and cheered when the lilac 1957 Chevy made its way onto the track.

A volunteer sign painter had transformed the car, and it now carried the red #4 and the man who made that number famous in this part of Illinois. Joe waved to the crowd, again. And they stood and cheered, again.

But then the car slowed and stopped on the back-stretch. No one wanted to say it aloud, but was the excitement too much for the old man? Maybe it was just a problem with the car. Or maybe the trauma of climbing into a stock car caused some injury to those brittle bones.

Suddenly, that lone car on the track roared back to life. It came through turns three and four with a power slide, right out of the '60s. Then the reason for the delay became clear. As the car flashed in front of the stands, a checkered flag waved from the passenger side window.

Somehow, Joe and a coconspirator had concealed an old reminder of his racing days in that blanket.

It was like a slow-motion scene in a movie. You could see his weak, crooked fingers holding the flag. You could see the smile on his face. And if you were as lucky as this writer, you could remember the times when this happened every Friday night. When the car returned to the pit gate, Joe seemed to slip out so much easier. It was as if he was already floating from the experience. His eyes were different, too. They sparkled again.

Dennis Yohnka

[AUTHOR'S NOTE: *After the racing season, the cars at the old Sugar Island Speedway were often dismantled and left in a junk-yard adjacent to the track. The lilac door with the red 4 was dis-covered there, and it hung proudly in the bedroom of this writer as a teenager.*]

The Tim Richmond Story

You could put Tim Richmond in a covered wagon, and if it would steer to the left, he would get the most of it. No doubt in my mind, Tim was the closest thing out there to Dale Earnhardt.

Crew Chief Larry McReynolds

Growing up in the Midwest, it seemed Tim Richmond was destined for stardom in the open-wheel ranks more popular in that era and area. He got a late start in racing, falling in love with the sport after taking a test drive in a friend's race car on a lark. In 1977, Tim showed up at Sandusky Speedway, the "fastest half-mile in Ohio" with a Super Modified car. Prior to the start of the race, Tim drove his car to the start/finish line, climbed up on top of the car's roof wing and greeted the crowd. He told them they might not know who he was, but they were going to learn his name real soon. And Tim was as good as his word. He won both Rookie of the Year and Track Champion honors in that car that year.

Tim's career detoured into stock-car racing in a rather unusual fashion. In 1980, Richmond won Rookie of the

Year honors at the Indianapolis 500. He had been in position to win the Indy 500 itself when his car ran out of gas. Race-winner Johnny Rutherford stopped and gave Tim a lift to Victory Circle on the side of his race car.

Among the hundreds of thousands of spectators at Indy that week were Doctors Joe and Rose Mattioli, who own the Pocono International Speedway. Impressed with Tim's driving prowess, they asked him if he might be interested in driving a stock car at their track later that year. When Tim accepted, the Mattiolis arranged for a car for him to drive. Tim Richmond finished twelfth in his first NASCAR Winston Cup race.

Tim enjoyed a lot of success at Pocono during his all-too-brief career, winning there four times. But my favorite Tim Richmond story involves something he did off the track at Pocono.

As he normally did, Tim was running late getting to driver introductions that morning. Also as normal, he was quickly surrounded by fans wanting an autograph. Tim did his best to accommodate everybody and still make it to the stage on time. That's when he noticed a little boy pulling on his pants leg, desperately trying to get Tim's attention. He had to be on stage, so Tim picked up that little boy and carried him up onto the platform while waving at the crowd with his free hand. The youngster was clearly overwhelmed by the roar of the crowd as they greeted Tim. Without missing a beat, Tim took the microphone and asked the young man, "Who is your favorite race-car driver?" The child immediately replied "Dale Earnhardt." Everyone burst out laughing, and Tim was laughing as hard as anyone else. Afterwards he carried the boy off the stage to return him to his parents. With everyone laughing that hard, the kid looked afraid, fearing he'd said something wrong. His parents doubtlessly were abashed. But as he set the boy down,

Tim leaned over and whispered, "Dale Earnhardt is my favorite race-car driver, too."

Richmond would enjoy his greatest success driving for Rick Hendrick with Harry Hyde as his crew chief. Folgers sponsored the car in that era, and the relationship nearly got off to a rocky start. Once again Tim overslept and was late for the sponsor press conference, one of the great sins of stock-car racing. But Tim managed to turn even that into a positive. As he sat down to greet the press, Tim was handed a badly needed cup of the sponsor's product. He took a gulp with evident enthusiasm and deadpanned, "If this stuff can wake me up at this hour, it can wake anyone up."

The year 1986 was destined to be Tim's greatest season. The year got off to a slow start, but late in the year Tim was all but unstoppable. In one twelve-race stretch, Tim won six times and finished second four more times. But for those close to him, there was a lot of concern for Tim, who didn't look too well in that period. We know now what was wrong, but originally it was thought that Tim had pneumonia. He'd find out that winter that his situation was far graver.

Tim had to sit out the first portion of the 1987 NASCAR season, but he returned to racing that June at Pocono. In a Hollywood ending that would make even a B-grade producer blush, Tim not only completed the race, but he won in resounding fashion. And the partisan Pocono crowd loudly welcomed back their hero. That afternoon Tim was at a rare loss for words, but he lingered just a little bit longer, soaking up the crowd's adulation. He knew his time was short.

One week later on Father's Day Tim won at Riverside, another track where he'd had great success. Tim was able to dedicate the win to his dad, Al. But that was destined to be his last race victory. Later that year with his health failing, Tim decided it was in the best interest of his team that he resign. On August 13, 1989, Tim Richmond passed away.

Maybe Dale Earnhardt really was Tim's favorite race-car driver as he told that little boy at Pocono, but Tim Richmond is and always will be my favorite driver.

Matt McLaughlin

An Athlete to Cheer For

The greater the obstacle, the more glory in over-coming it.

Moliere

We've reached the point of annoyance with spoiled athletes—those with bad attitudes who don't want to sign autographs, who don't want to talk with the media about anything besides how great they are. Oh, and don't forget those who complain about their futures when they have a year left on a $10 million deal, or hold out of training camp while signed to a $3.5 million-a-year contract.

If you're one of the people who has had it with athletes, this story will give you a reason to cheer.

Imagine being a sixteen-year-old girl and feeling numbness on the right side of your body. Imagine going to a doctor, and after undergoing a spinal tap and an MRI, you find out that you have multiple sclerosis (MS). Imagine basically being sentenced to a wheelchair for the rest of your life. That's the life story of Kelly Sutton, except she refused to be confined to a wheelchair. Now at age thirty-one, Kelly does a lot of sitting, though—in a race car.

Kelly is a third-generation race-car driver who began racing go-carts at a dirt track in her hometown of Crownsville, Maryland, at the age of twelve. Her dream since she was five was to one day race at Daytona International Speedway.

When the MS diagnosis was made, all of her racing dreams were put on hold for a few years. However, with the support of her family, therapy and medication, Kelly came back to the track. "I decided I was going to live every day and do everything I could to be proud of what I've done," she said. "I'm not going to waste my life lying around saying, 'I have MS.'"

From 1992 to 1994, she raced on the Old Dominion Speedway in the Pro Mini-Stock Series. She won seven feature races, twenty qualifiers and five pole positions. She was voted the Most Popular Driver all three years on the series and received the Metropolitan Auto Racing Fan Club of Maryland, Delaware, and Virginia Award in 1994—an award very special to Sutton because it was also won by her grandfather and father.

In 1997, she became the first woman to win regionally or nationally on the Allison National Legacy Series. She won two feature races and three pole positions on the Allison Legacy Pennsylvania Series that same year.

In 1998, she won one qualifying race and the Oral B Close Brush Award on the Parts Pro Truck Series, and in 2000, she moved up to the Goody's Dash Series, NASCAR Touring Division. She competed in two races in 2000 with a season-best sixteenth-place finish.

Then, in February 2001, Kelly's childhood dream was realized as she raced at Daytona International Speedway. "It was awesome, and it was intimidating," Sutton said. "I've raced short tracks for ten years, but you can throw everything you've learned out the window at the Speedway. I was on pins and needles, but it felt great."

Sutton returned to Daytona in July 2001 to race in the DaytonaUSA.com 150. She was running second for a while and was in the top five throughout the race before a late accident dropped her to twenty-seventh place. "I couldn't wait to get that season over with, to get back to Daytona and race there again," she said.

Usually taking things one year at a time, Kelly debated whether or not to race full time in 2002. The last time she'd raced full-time was on her local tracks, so she was gone on Saturday mornings and home in the evening. Now she was concerned about the toll it might take on her body. "I'm not willing to put everything on the line for racing," she admitted.

But after taking everything into consideration, Kelly and her team gave the full-time schedule a go-ahead for the 2002 season. Of course, she doesn't do anything halfway, and once Kelly decided the full season was a go, she immediately set her goal on winning the Goody's Dash Series Rookie-of-the-Year. She finished third, just fifteen points off the lead, in the final Rookie-of-the-Year standings. She also placed a solid twelfth in the overall season standings. She not only returned to Daytona in 2002, but she finished a very strong eleventh at the February race.

The 2002 year came to an official close with the season-ending celebration at the Greensboro Convention Center in North Carolina. There Kelly walked away with the Most Popular Driver Award. "I was really surprised when they called my name out," she beemed. "It was a wonderful feeling."

So you think Kelly Sutton has any plans to slow down? Forget that! She will not only run the full 2003 Goody's Dash Series season, but she's also going to try and compete in a few NASCAR Craftsman Truck Series races. Her other goals for 2003? "To finish in the top five in points (in the Goody's Dash Series standings) and win a race."

Kelly takes a medication called Copaxone®, which helps reduce the frequency of relapses in people with multiple sclerosis. Individual results can vary, but since June 1999, Sutton has suffered only one relapse. She now races for Team COPAXONE®, which was established in 2000. The team celebrates the accomplishments of people like Sutton who refuse to let MS stand in their way.

"I want to be a role model for people with MS and show that life doesn't stop," Kelly says. "If I go into a wheelchair in the next five years, I'm going to be proud of what I've done."

She's an athlete who's easy to cheer for.

Andrew Kossak

Twenty-Five Cents at a Time

Keep true to the dreams of thy youth.

Johann Friedrich Von Schiller

You'll see Don Prudhomme leaning over the engine of his NHRA Miller Top Fuel dragster to give a piece of advice to his young driver, Larry Dixon.

On the Winston Cup/NASCAR circuit, Felix Sabates leaves his far-flung business interests to offer support to his Coors/Pontiac driver Kyle Petty.

That's sports and especially the norm for a race-car owner.

But here's an owner who won't be near when his black Camaro fires up for a Late Model Sportsman heat or a feature at Columbia Motorsports Park (CMP).

Even when the green flag falls, this owner will be as helpless in his team's effort as any other spectator in row nine of the nondrinking grandstand.

He's not allowed in the pits.

The reason?

The owner of David Johnson's #98 Camaro has not been banned for fighting. He wasn't suspended for bringing alcohol into the pits, and it isn't that he doesn't have the infield admission price, even though most of his resources went into the car.

No, Michael James Johnson is just eight years old, and since CMP rules you must be at least fourteen to enter the infield, even if you're a car owner, he must watch from afar.

Yes, young Johnson, hereafter referred to as Mike, is realizing a dream of many three and four times his age.

Did you read what I'm saying? Mike, an A student at Old Town Elementary School, is the owner of record, not just sentiment, of his dad's car.

To fully appreciate the story, we'll listen to veteran driver Johnson. Senior, that is.

"I raced first enduro and then Pure Stock and Hobby Stock at Bronson from about 1993 until 1998, while Mike was still in diapers. I'd take him to Victory Lane whenever I won a race.

"Then my wife, Carolyn, and I were divorced, and I had to give up racing. But she's probably the best ex-wife a man's ever had," Johnson said. "She doesn't live far from me in Chiefland, and Michael spends a whole lot of time at my shop (Johnson's Garage and Body Shop).

"It broke his heart when I had to give up racing."

Indeed, Mike's love of racing followed him out of those diapers, to his first steps and farther. It was only natural he wanted to see his dad back in a race car, even if it required him buying one. That's right—that wasn't a typo.

"Two or three years ago, he started saying, 'Dad, let's get a race car. I'll buy it,'" Johnson said. "You can imagine what I said to that. 'Yeah right. We'll see. Maybe one day.'"

That one day came sooner than Johnson had figured possible. When David Johnson's sister, Nancy, passed away, Mike inherited a two-foot ceramic frog in the likeness of Kermit. It was also his aunt's bank, and he started putting all his loose change in it every day. That went on for several years, and, at the close of each day, after school, or visiting and helping his dad at the shop, Mike would toss his change into the bank.

"He answers the phone, chases wrenches, sweeps up, anything he can do at the shop," Johnson said. "He just loves being there.

"About last September, he came to me again and said he wanted us to buy a race car, that he had the money in Kermit. I still thought, *Yeah, sure. How much money could be in that frog?*

"Well, he rolled it in—it was too heavy to try and carry—and started emptying the coins out of it. He wouldn't break it because he is not a destructive youngster at all.

"Well, he filled up both halves of one of those big turkey roasting pans. It took almost two hours.

"I said, 'This is your money. Are you sure this is what you want to do with it?' And he insisted it was."

Before they went to the bank, his mom came by to pick up Mike for a trip to Wal-Mart, and he was urged to take some of the money, in case he saw something that caught his fancy. "He took just two quarters," Johnson said. He said, 'This is for the race car.'"

With Mike's money, between eight hundred and nine hundred dollars, Johnson and longtime friend Mike Miller and the potential car owner, purchased a rolling chassis in November.

From there, it was a matter of finishing up the Sportsman car. Miller and friends pitched in to help, a group effort.

"I told Mike (we call him Mighty Mike), 'We need to put your name on the car. Where do you want it?' He said, 'Don't make it very large, because we need the room for sponsors. Put it on the back.'"

As well as his dad, Mike used to follow the racing success of Newberry's Ricky Rain, who, after a hiatus, has returned to Late Model Sportsman ranks at CMP.

Mike said he wanted this car to look just like Ricky's black, and even down to the #98, which was Ricky's. Since he wasn't driving at the time, Ricky said that was fine.

Mike has, indeed, left room for other sponsors on the car, but underneath the "Thank You Mighty Mike" salute on the back is a bumper sticker placed there by the driver. It reads Proud Parent of an Old Town Elementary Semester Honor Roll Student.

Johnson said with his straight A's, Mike probably should be in an advanced class, perhaps even skip a grade, but that's not provided for in the school.

So, for now, he's a third grader who is also a car owner.

One night during an open practice without any racing, Mike was busy rubbing down the right side and cleaning the windshield of his #98 Camaro.

The eight-year-old also fetched a wrench when asked by Miller or his dad.

Whoa. You can't get in the pits unless you're fourteen. What's the deal?

Since it was simply open practice, with no grandstand admission, Team Johnson figured it would be okay if Mighty Mike spent a night in the pits.

Please don't tell CMP officials. Mike simply lay down on the floor of the tow truck and pulled his dad's driving suit over him.

When complimented on the appearance of his car, Mike grinned and said, "Thanks."

"But what about the driver? Are you happy with the driver?" he was asked.

"Yeah," he shyly grinned.

"He'd better say that, because it's a long way back to Cleveland," his dad said.

Oh, the stress of being a car owner.

Norm Froscher

Win One for Me, Daddy

The 1987 season was a tough year. Up to that point, I was at the top of the world of racing. I had won three NASCAR Winston Cup championships. I had won about seventy races in NASCAR Winston Cup and many poles. Racing had been very good to me. But in 1987, I was with a new team, and things weren't going very well. It had been expected that this new team would go gangbusters. We were the dream team. I had the best of backing from the Hendrick Motorsports Group, an excellent sponsorship, and the best engine builder in racing. However, going into the last part of the season, we still had not won a race. This had not happened to me since I got my first NASCAR Winston Cup win in 1975.

In addition to my not winning races, we found out that Stevie, my wife, was pregnant. All of this was emotionally tough for me. Stevie had three miscarriages previously, including one in 1986. She had never been able to carry a baby to full term, and I felt badly for her. I leaned on her so much. She is my best friend and had always been with me at every race.

Now she was not able to go to the track each weekend with me. That was difficult. Stevie has always been such a part of my life and my racing career. We had always gone to races together. I had not experienced life at the track without Stevie. I have been deeply in love with her since we met in high school back in Owensboro, Kentucky. She has stood by me with much encouragement through the ups and downs and boos and cheers of fans. She had set a new standard in racing by being a part of my race team on Sundays at a time when women were not allowed in the pits. It was tough on me to be racing without her there.

On September 17, we were blessed with our first child, Jessica Leigh. We were very excited! I had to leave to go on to the next race later that week. The race was at Martinsville, Virginia, where I had won several times before. But I had no expectations of winning this time.

As the race progressed I really had no hope of winning, as I was a lap down with just twenty-five laps to go. Dale Earnhardt was leading. When he stopped for fuel, I got back on the lead lap. Then a caution came out with about seven laps to go. On the restart, I was in third place behind Earnhardt and Terry Labonte. Both of these guys were previous champions and were tough, hard racers. There was no way I was going to get by them with just a few laps to go. They could make it very difficult to get around them. On the final lap in the final turns of 3 and 4, Terry had gotten up beside Dale and left just a little opening for me to pass both of them, beating them to the finish line. I won my first race of the year!

It was much more special, though, than just being my first win of the season and my first victory with the new team. For earlier that Sunday morning, appearing from nowhere, I was surprised to find a little rosebud in the seat of my car with a note that said, "Win one for me, Daddy!" My first race of the season was sweetened by it occurring on the same day that I was first called "Daddy."

Darrell Waltrip with Max Helton

Learning from Dylan

Riverhead Raceway, a NASCAR-sanctioned track, is a tight quarter-mile facility that runs up to six classes on any given Saturday. Those divisions are the Blunderbust, Charger, Late Model, Super Pro Truck, Figure Eight and Modified. The Modified division is the featured division. A demolition derby or other novelty attraction may be scheduled on any given night. In the summer of 2000, we (the local division of Racing 4 Kids Charities) decided to host a night at the races for a child and his or her family.

The child chosen was eight-year-old Dylan Hronec, who was brought to our attention by Henry "The Phantom" Cataldo and his crew chief Kenny Webber. Dylan has cerebral palsy. Webber was by trade a contractor, who met Dylan while working at Dylan's home, installing a handicapped ramp. Webber had observed Dylan playing with a toy Matchbox race car, rolling it down the ramp.

After watching the boy play for a while, Kenny asked if Dylan was a race fan. An excited Dylan quickly answered "yes." After work, Webber relayed the story to his race team at the team's shop.

Soon after, Henry stopped by to meet Dylan at his home. Dylan proved to be a very friendly, intelligent, upbeat young man with a positive disposition, despite the disability that life gave him. When the day arrived, Dylan, along with his brother Gregg and his parents, met us outside the back spectator gate, where we proceeded inside the facility. Once inside, we found our seats behind the starter's stand by the start/finish line.

Dylan's family was provided with free admission, dinner, souvenirs and munchies throughout the evening. Many drivers, crewmembers, car owners and track officials made the long trek from the pit area to the spectator area to greet Dylan and his family, some giving him team T-shirts and autographed pictures. During the week leading up to the races, several teams even had special messages for Dylan placed on their race cars.

During the evening, the track announcer, Bob Finan, came down from the press box to say hello to Dylan and his family. The announcer also asked Dylan to help with the NASCAR Modified Victory Lane presentation.

At one point, driver Kevin Metzger won the evening's Late Model feature race. During the Victory Lane ceremony, Kevin acknowledged Dylan over the track public-address system. After he pulled his car out of Victory Lane and off the track, a track employee came up to where we were all sitting.

"Where's Dylan?" he asked. After being pointed out, the track worker handed the winner's trophy to the stunned Dylan.

"Kevin Metzger asked me to give this to you," he told the happy and surprised youngster.

Later that evening, Chuck Steuer won the Modified feature. Dylan was brought down on to the track, where he helped Bob Finan with the Victory Lane celebration.

"Congratulations!" Dylan said as he presented the

trophy to Steuer. There were many photos taken of Dylan and Steuer in Victory Lane, as well as videos by track photographers.

Henry Cataldo, Kenny Webber, and other drivers and officials came onto the track unknown to Dylan, as he was busy with the celebrations. When everyone was together, we called Dylan over to where we had gathered.

"Dylan," I said over the public-address system, "on behalf of Henry Cataldo, Kenny Webber, John Wellman of Big Brothers and Big Sisters of Long Island, all of the drivers in the Modified division, the Riverhead Raceway officials, promoters Barbara and Jim Cromarty, and Racing 4 Kids, we'd like to present you with this helmet, which was signed by all of the Modified drivers who have been at Riverhead Raceway in the last three weeks."

The stunned youngster said "Thank you" as he stared at the helmet in disbelief, while thousands in attendance applauded. It was both heartwarming and surprising to watch the competitors, officials and Dylan's parents who were standing trackside, all with tears in their eyes. And there sat Dylan with an ear-to-ear grin, his head capped with his new autographed helmet, holding the trophy that was given to him.

In the weeks following, we received a package from Dylan containing pictures, drawings and notes of appreciation from him and his family. My wife and I were left with a feeling of complete joy, knowing that Dylan was able to experience something so wonderful. We were trying to show Dylan that there were people out there who really care, and who want to help. But Dylan already knew that; the lesson was one that the rest of us learned.

Mike Fields

It's Not All About Sunday

*Nothing is so potent as the silent influence of a
good example.*

James Kent

People often wonder what it is about racing that seems
to get into the hearts of race fans. After all, aren't they just
going around and around in circles? Surely there isn't
much talent in that, so what can possibly hold a race fan's
interest? In one respect, it's *all* about Sunday. In another,
it has nothing at all to do with Sunday.

There are as many different kinds of race fans as there
are paint schemes on a race car. Some people follow the
manufacturer and will go to their graves hating Ford or
Chevy out of allegiance for the other. There are those old-
timer fans who have been around since the Saturday
nights on dirt, and who have spent their lives hating a guy
named Earnhardt or Waltrip just because of an accident
involving their own favorite driver back in 1975. Then
there are the sentimental fans. They are the ones who root
for a guy who has raced 462 races and never won. They
root for a guy because his brother was killed at the

racetrack. They root for another guy because he had a head injury and nobody would hire him for two years. Those are the great stories of racing, and there are a thousand more just like them.

I'm a sentimental race fan. I don't much care about twenty-five years ago, nor do I even know what manufacturer every team drives. But I do know stories about people. I know about a man named Bobby who lost two sons in two years, and then in his grief, lost his wife, Judy, to divorce. But I keep watching because I know that a few years later, in helping another father through the same grief, he was remarried to Judy, the only woman he really loved.

Week after week, when I see a car spin and hit the wall, it isn't just a machine, it's a friend—someone whose personal life I know about. If a guy named Ward crashes, I wonder if a son named Jeb might be worried. When a driver named Michael wins his first race, I wonder just how much the heart of a wife named Buffy might be bursting with pride. When a guy named Dale dies, I wonder how a daughter named Taylor will grow up having lost the most important man who will ever be a part of her life.

Do I wonder these things because of how I admire the ability to drive in circles at 190 miles per hour? No. I wonder these things because I admire the men who place family above racing. I admire these sports heroes who go to church on Sunday and aren't ever arrested for drug abuse or wife beating. I admire the man we call DJ who devotes a great deal of time and money toward breast-cancer research, and another named Darrell who has a weekly Bible study in his garage for a couple hundred men every week, even when he's out of town.

The next time you watch forty-three cars running around a track in a circle and wonder why anyone would watch, just sit back and listen for a while. Hear the stories of the men who are driving these cars, look for their wives and children cheering them on, and remind yourself that it's not all about Sunday.

Carol Einarsson

Special Delivery

Amber Lynn loved to read and sing to her younger sister, Crystal, and she also enjoyed watching NASCAR racing with her dad. Because United Parcel Service (UPS) sponsors driver Dale Jarrett, Amber's favorite commercial for the "big brown truck" would frequently appear during the races. Whenever she spotted the brown delivery truck in her neighborhood, Amber Lynn would squeal, "Mommy, Mommy, look—the big brown truck!" and a wide smile would cross her face. For Amber, watching for the delivery truck had become a daily routine. When the precious four-year-old died from complications of Byler's disease (a rare liver ailment), her family and friends were distraught. Her grandmother contacted UPS and related to them Amber's story.

Tim, a UPS employee, responded to the call. On the day of her burial, Tim parked his big brown delivery truck directly in front of the funeral parlor. He quietly walked toward Amber's casket and reverently placed inside it a UPS teddy bear and a model of the big brown truck that Amber Lynn had loved so dearly. Then he said, "These are for Crystal" as he presented to Amber's parents a company pen and stuffed doggie. As he walked back down the aisle, Amber's parents watched tears slowly roll down Tim's face. He drove his big brown delivery truck in the funeral procession to the cemetery. Upon Amber's grave, Tim placed a small box with a rose on top and Crystal was told, "This special box is for you. It is filled with hugs, kisses and love from your big sister Amber."

A few days after the funeral, Sue, another UPS driver, delivered a model big brown truck to Amber's family for Crystal. Sue would accept no payment for this special delivery but instead she simply replied, "I can afford it; this is something I want to do." Now Crystal would have a model big brown truck to play with just like the one her big sister Amber would be playing with in heaven.

Dale Jarrett heard about Amber's story, and he sent a beautiful bereavement message to her family. But he did more than that. Dale pinned Amber's picture to the dashboard of his car, and as he drove laps around the track during a fall NASCAR race, the national audience saw Amber's sweet face flash across the television screen. They listened as the NASCAR announcer told how Amber Lynn's kidneys were donated to two different children. And they learned of another precious child (somewhere in Ohio) who sings and reads with the heart of Amber Lynn beating inside her. Amber Lynn became an organ donor so that others might live; now all would know.

To Amber's family, Dale Jarrett had delivered more than a winning performance. And Tim and Sue had delivered more than packages. They delivered love.

Susan J. Siersma

Reprinted by permission of Mike Smith, Las Vegas Sun.

A NASCAR® Wish

How do you begin a letter to a widow you've never met? thought Rob Quillen as he sat at his keyboard.

How do you tell the wife of one of the pilots who perished in the terrorist hijackings that only a day earlier you and he had become fast friends, bonded by family stories, a love for NASCAR and a crazy devotion to Jeff Gordon?

And how can we get the pilot's son to Kansas City for Sunday's race?

Should I even write a letter?

Quillen turned to his wife, Sue Anne, and asked whether she would want to hear from a stranger who happened to be the last person to enjoy a long conversation with her husband.

"Absolutely," she said.

Dear Dahl Family,

I must start this letter by saying how sorry I am about your loss. Like all America, my heart goes out to you. I know you do not know me, nor do I know you.

The business trip on September 10 did not start well for Quillen, an account executive for Automatic Data Processing in Lincoln, Nebraska. He was bumped from his

New York–bound flight and bused to Omaha to catch another. This journey would take him first to Denver and then to Newark, New Jersey.

Quillen, wearing a Jeff Gordon shirt and counting down the days to his trip to the Protection One 400 at Kansas Speedway on September 30, shuffled onto his United flight in Denver. He settled into his seat for hours of pecking on the laptop.

Then the flight attendant came by and offered open rows to the passengers that were seated next to Quillen. *Great,* Quillen thought, *his own row.* But the aisle seat was quickly taken by a gentleman who, before buckling his seat belt, asked Quillen about his shirt.

"Do you work for Jeff Gordon?" the passenger asked.

"No, just a big fan," Quillen said.

"Yeah, my son and I are, too."

And that's how the conversation got started. Back and forth it went. Jeff Gordon, Monte Carlo, NASCAR, Kansas Speedway. All the essential Gordon topics were covered before the plane reached cruising altitude. The flight attendant handed a beer to Quillen's new friend, who did not reach for his wallet.

"How did you pull that off?" Quillen asked. "You're either very important, or you're dating her."

"Neither," Jason Dahl said. "I'm a pilot. I've got the Newark-to-San Francisco morning flight tomorrow. I'm just catching a ride out there."

The next day Dahl, captain aboard United Flight 93, would perish with forty-four others in a rural Pennsylvania field, the last of four hijacked airplanes to crash on a terror-filled morning.

Profiles of victims had become a daily news staple, and stories of the heroism about the passengers and crew aboard Flight 93 are beginning to emerge. The plane was headed for more destruction, probably to Washington.

For some reason it never reached its destination.

It was very obvious that Jason loved his family, his life, his job. He spoke of you several times; he spoke of your recent anniversary and some of the trips he had taken with his son.

Dahl asked the attendant to bring his buddy a beer, and Quillen's laptop never left its case. They laughed and talked about their jobs and families. Quillen told Dahl about Sue Anne and their two young children.

Dahl talked about how he and his wife, Sandy, a flight attendant, had just celebrated an anniversary, and how much fun the family had taking trips with Dahl's son, fifteen-year-old Matt.

They barely knew each other, but Quillen felt comfortable enough to ask Dahl something he could never remember asking a fellow traveler.

"Hypothetically speaking, say your life ended tomorrow, what would be the last thing you'd want to do?"

"I'd want to go to a NASCAR race," Dahl said. "I'd want to see Jeff Gordon race, and I'd want to meet him with my son."

Quillen knew he was about to make Dahl happy.

"I'm doing this customer appreciation thing at the track in Kansas City, and I've got a couple of extra tickets. You want to go?"

Dahl pulled out his planner.

"I've got something on the 29th. But we'll catch an early-morning flight on the 30th and come home that night."

"Great. Give me a phone number and address, and when I get home to Nebraska, I'll send you the tickets."

Dahl asked how much they'd cost. "Don't worry about it," Quillen said.

They exchanged business cards. Dahl scribbled his cell number on the back of his.

Dahl thought for a moment and came up with a way to return the favor. He's in charge of flight simulator time for United in Denver, near his home in Littleton, Colorado. "Next time you come out there, I'll let you land a 757 in Tokyo. It's the best video game in the world."

Dahl checked his watch. Approaching 8 P.M. No second beer. Regulations. But the conversation carried on. Quillen learned about airports where landing was difficult. Flying in bad weather. Engine failure. Just about everything a pilot dreads.

They certainly didn't talk about hijackings. That just doesn't happen anymore.

If it's possible to become close friends in four hours, Jason and I accomplished this.

News of a fire at the World Trade Center broke up Quillen's meeting at the New Jersey hotel just off the George Washington Bridge. Quillen headed inside to call Sue Anne.

Then he heard people yelling, "Look, look, look!" Quillen turned his head in time to see a fireball blast from the side of the second tower.

Quillen raced back to call Sue Anne, but all phone service was out. Soon came word of the Pentagon disaster, and another plane crash in Pennsylvania.

The meetings were canceled. Quillen's co-workers found television sets and were searching for more information when a friend told Quillen he heard that one of the downed planes originated in Newark.

"It didn't hit me at first," Quillen said. "Then, all of a sudden I realized."

Quillen ran to his room and found Dahl's business card. He called the cell number on the back, begging Dahl to pick up. But the call was transferred to the pilot's voice mail.

I am not sure if any of you have access to his voice mail on his cell phone, but I was the one that left the long message, crying, and telling Jason and his family, God bless you all. I am sorry for that message if you do get it. I was very emotional when I left that message.

Like all of America's airline travelers, Quillen was stranded. One group was headed in a rental car to Texas, another to Minnesota. That did not help Quillen, who heard that perhaps there would be flights out of the Manchester, New Hampshire, airport. That's where his group went.

The terminal was packed. A United representative jumped on the counter, announced there would be no flights out until Monday. This was Friday. Quillen hustled to the Hertz counter, told them he was headed to Lincoln, filled out the paperwork and headed west. He told his wife he'd be home on Saturday, and at 11:55 P.M. that day he walked through his front door.

For the next few days Quillen was consumed by the idea of getting Matt Dahl to Kansas City so the teenager could meet Jeff Gordon. But how? Quillen can quote chapter and verse on Gordon, from his Ford Thunderbird days on the NASCAR Busch Series circuit through his phenomenal years with the NASCAR Winston Cup.

Quillen has a "24 CAR" Nebraska license plate on his red Monte Carlo with the plate border from Gordon's Wilmington, North Carolina, dealership.

But none of that gets Quillen any closer to Gordon. Quillen had seen him up close, gotten pit passes, but was no more than a distant devotee like countless others.

So he just took a chance. The same day he sent the letter to Sandy Dahl, he fired off an e-mail to Gordon. The next day he got a response from Gordon's public-relations firm that made him ecstatic.

"Please extend an invitation to Jason's family to attend the

DuPont hospitality tent next Sunday morning at Kansas Speedway," wrote Jon Edwards, Gordon's publicity director. "We will give them a tour and make sure they experience life in the garage area leading up to a NASCAR Winston Cup race. We will also set up a meeting with Jeff." That was on Thursday. On Friday, Quillen got another message, this one on the telephone.

"You wouldn't believe it," Quillen said Friday. "I've talked to Jeff Gordon and (NASCAR Winston Cup team owner) Rick Hendrick today. They can't wait to meet Matt."

But would the Dahl family be there? Quillen had not heard. He didn't have the family's home phone number. He had sent his letter in overnight mail and knew it arrived late Thursday morning. Maybe Sandy Dahl wasn't responding to anybody.

Then Quillen got the call. Jason Dahl's funeral was Thursday in Littleton, and Sandy could not reach Quillen until Friday.

"I told him his letter gave me the happiest feeling, and it made Matt happy as well," Sandy Dahl said. "There were so many wonderful things in it. I'm so grateful he decided to contact me. I'll always cherish that letter."

She then gave Quillen the good news. She was working on arrangements to send Matt and his grandfather to Kansas City.

Matt, it turns out, is a veteran racing observer. He and his father loved going to the Indianapolis 500. They had planned on visiting as many tracks together as possible. Sandy wasn't surprised to hear that her husband was lining up a trip to Kansas Speedway.

Know in your heart that Jason is in a better place, and that he is looking down on us watching now. He would want us to be strong and continue on.

Perhaps the most popular driver on the NASCAR Winston Cup circuit, Jeff Gordon receives hundreds of fan requests every month. He has heard a lot of touching stories. But Rob Quillen's plea stood out.

"You don't realize sometimes how big our sport is, and we're starting to see just how wide-scale this tragedy is," Gordon said Saturday, after his practice run for Sunday's race in Dover, Delaware. "It's one story after another about people being affected by this.

"I had said I didn't really know anybody or didn't have any family or close friends I knew of who were directly affected by this, but this does affect me, that there was someone out there who was a big fan who had a son who is such a big fan.

"So we're going to do all we can. We probably would have tried to meet this little boy no matter what, but we're certainly going to try to do everything we can to put a smile on his face right now, because I know he's going through a tough time."

Gordon has already given some thought to how he will spend time with Matt Dahl at this weekend's race. He'll take him to a hospitality tent, attend chapel services and escort him to pre-race driver introductions.

"I'll ask him, 'Is there any question you have for me, any picture you want, any autograph you want? . . . Whatever it is you'd like to do within reason—besides riding with me, maybe—we're going to do everything we can.'"

Gordon hopes to keep in touch with Matt beyond Sunday.

"Different people touch our lives in different ways, and we touch people's lives in different ways," said Gordon, "and if there's a way a bond and friendship can be made out of that, that will be great."

I have no idea why I was placed next to Jason that night. . . . The only clear thing I understand is that God wants me to work all of this out so that your family can come to the race, and your son gets an opportunity to meet Jeff Gordon and watch him race.

"My father-in-law said there must have been thousands of people flying that day, and what are the odds that Jason would sit next to me?" Quillen said. "I wasn't even supposed to be on that flight.

"Maybe somebody knew this was going to happen, and that's why we were together. Maybe I'm the person who is supposed to help his son meet Jeff Gordon. I don't know. But when I got back, I knew I'd feel terrible if I didn't at least try to get this done."

Blair Kerkhoff

Father's Day 1973

The 1973 Daytona 500 probably doesn't top most fans' lists as the greatest running of the real Great American Race. Its outcome was not decided by a last-lap wreck like the classic 1976 or '79 events, nor did it feature two drivers nose to tail heading for the finish as in '93 or '96. But it is, and always will be, the most memorable running of the February classic in my book, because it was the first NASCAR event I attended. My dad took me.

I had been a fan of stock-car racing since I was five years old, though living in the Northeast, coverage was spotty at best, limited to an occasional segment of a race shown on ABC's *Wide World of Sports*, or a small blurb in the newspaper Monday morning I would reread a dozen times. Nor do I come from a family involved in any way with the sport. In fact my preoccupation with fast, loud cars was considered a bit worrisome, and everyone hoped it was just a phase I was going through. To be truthful, I guess some of the family is still waiting for me to outgrow it.

Dad wore a tie seven days a week, even on weekends, and to him a great Saturday or Sunday afternoon was relaxing in a recliner, reading a novel or *The New York Times*. He always watched *Wide World of Sports,* no matter what was on, as a creature of habit. If stock-car racing came on, he'd bury himself back in the *Times* and try to ignore my cheering and occasional leaping about.

Fast forward to 1973. I was thirteen years old, and like many boys that age, a bit of a trial, smart-mouthed, cynical and difficult, and still very much a gearhead, of course. Dad announced he had a special surprise for the family shortly after Christmas at Sunday breakfast. He was taking my mom, my four sisters and me to Disney World. My sisters were thrilled. I rolled my eyes, and announced I had no intention of going on such a lame kid's trip to see a giant rat. I asked if I could stay with a friend instead. Not the sort of reaction Dad was hoping for. I continued my campaign to be allowed to stay home until Dad made another surprise announcement a couple of weeks later. If I would go along on the Florida vacation and promise not to be a pest, he would take me to see the Daytona 500 while we were down there. I may have been the first person in history to scream, "I'm going to Disney World!"

I recall hearing Dad tell Mom that he was surprised how expensive seats were for the race, but Dad was the sort of man that if he gave his word he kept it. I don't think Dad had any idea just how big a deal the 500 was. When we arrived at Disney World that Friday, he picked up a phone book and called Hertz to arrange for a rental car. Of course none were available. Same deal at Avis, Budget and the rest. Someone finally explained to Dad that it was Speed Weeks and there was not a single rental car to be had in the state of Florida. Dad was not a man to shy away from a challenge so he even resorted to trying Ryder, U-Haul and other truck rental places, looking for anything with an engine and wheels that would get us to Daytona. No deal. Meanwhile I had grabbed the phone book in despair, thinking my trip to the race was about to be canceled. I pointed out one agency Dad hadn't tried.

The ad listed "Dune Buggies for Rent." For those of you who have forgotten, dune buggies were horrible, misshapen little fiberglass abominations every bit as embarrassing to recall as '70s haircuts, clothing and music. With great reluctance, Dad made the call. The rental agent said while they had thought the whole fleet was rented, the mechanics had just finished repairing one, and it would indeed be available. They could even drop it off at our hotel in the Magic Kingdom Sunday morning. When Dad suggested 10:30, the guy laughed and told him, "Mister, if you're going to the 500, you better plan on leaving a lot earlier than that, unless you're going to next year's race, I mean."

Sunday morning I woke up to a torrential downpour of the sort they never show in Florida tourism ads. And in fact the weather forecast was not good for the rest of the day, with heavy rain supposed to linger until the next morning. While we were waiting outside for our chariot, a guy told Dad and me not to worry. It never rained out the Daytona 500. Bill France had a special arrangement with the Man Upstairs. Of course, he probably would have sounded a lot more believable had he not been in a Mickey Mouse costume.

Our rental unit finally arrived, and I recall Dad gasping as he saw it. Not only was it a dune buggy, but it was hot pink, with a flowered roof and oversized tires mounted on purple painted rims. Dad was aghast. I thought it was the coolest thing I had ever seen. Dad tried to negotiate for a more sedate-looking blue unit that had served as a demo for the rental agent, but he explained that was his boss's private vehicle, despite an offer of a large bribe. My sisters were as delighted as I was by the beautiful pink car, but for some reason Mom was laughing out loud. She pointed her camera as Dad attempted to climb aboard. He looked at her and said in a voice that showed he was clearly not amused, "You take that picture and you may well end up divorced before this trip is over." I think he was kidding.

And so it was off to Daytona in our pink dune buggy, driving along rain-soaked stretches of interstates. Dad, of course, was wearing suit pants, a starched white shirt and a skinny tie, which had some other drivers stealing second looks. While I professed to be an expert on cars, I had some insane notion dune buggies were fast. Not with a VW engine they weren't. We got passed by everything on the road including, I seem to recall, a couple of grannies in Gremlins on their way to Sunday service. The roof leaked copious amounts of water into the car's interior. The defrosters didn't work, so I was assigned the task of keeping the windshield clear with my windbreaker's sleeve. The exhaust note was a loud, unpleasant tone not dissimilar to the sound one might expect to issue from the south end of a large hog facing north that had been rooting in the bean fields all night.

Conversation required screaming.

"Cool car, huh, Dad?" I bellowed. "Can we get one someday?"

Dad's stare made it hard to believe there would ever be such a vehicle in the McLaughlin family garage. Traffic was pretty bad, but as we waited to get into the lot the rains stopped. With race time approaching, I was constantly checking my watch and growing nervous. When we finally parked, we had to jog through the mud to get to our seats on time. Not much of a problem for me in my high-top Converses, but a bit of a challenge for Dad in his wing tips, which were to end up in the trash that night. When I first saw the track, I was knocked speechless, which anyone who knew me then will tell you took some doing. It was so huge it was beyond my imagining, with those high-banked corners that looked like walls and that big old lake in the center. Even Dad was impressed. Our seats were one section to the left of the start/finish line only three rows up from the fence. There were no jet dryers in those days, so tow trucks were dragging tires around to dry the track, as the crowd hustled to their seats. We ended up with some stereotypical good ol' boys sitting right behind us, a bit intoxicated even before the race began. One noticed my hand-lettered "43 Richard Petty" T-shirt (there were no souvenir T-shirts in those days) and slapped me on my back congratulating me on my wise choice.

Then he offered me a beer. Dad about died. I thanked the man as politely as I could, but explained I was too young to drink, which set the whole crew to laughing.

"Where you from, boy?" one of them asked me.

"Pennsylvania," I told him.

"Pennsylvania?" he asked, laughing even louder. "There a lot of race fans in Pennsylvania, are there?"

"Just me," I explained, which caused him to laugh so hard beer came out his nose, the first time I'd ever seen that trick done.

If seeing the track for the first time was a thrill, it was nothing compared to when the cars took to the track for the pace laps. The colors were so much brighter than on television. The sweet thunder of unmuffled race engines echoed around the track, and not those small block engines like they use today either. The real deal. Chrysler Hemis. Boss 429s. Chevy Rats. It was a sound you felt as much as heard and a sweet music like we may never hear again. In those days the drivers wore open-faced helmets so you could see their faces as they prepared to do battle. Most looked steely-eyed and determined. Richard was smiling and occasionally waving at the crowd, seemingly as relaxed as if he was going for a Sunday drive. And when the green dropped and forty cars accelerated wide open for that first turn, that music reached such a crescendo that at that very moment I became hooked for life on stock-car racing. The whole crowd rose to their feet cheering. Well, everyone but Dad, who thought such a display a bit unseemly.

Buddy Baker in his orange K and K Dodge was the class of the field that day, seemingly ready to lap the field. Country singer Marty Robbins in his purple and yellow Dodge crashed right in front of us, and I remember the wide-eyed look of panic in his eyes as he drilled the wall and spun by us. At one point Richard almost got lapped and my heart sank, but a well-timed yellow saved him from going a lap down. With twelve laps to go, Richard came into the pits for a splash of gas. There were no speed limits on pit road back then, and he kept the STP Dodge floored until the last moment, then locked up his brakes, smoke billowing off all four tires and skidding directly into his pits, lined up perfectly. Baker had to pit for fuel as well, and his stop took a bit longer. Petty was in the lead, but Baker was reeling him in, closing noticeably on every lap, and the laps were winding down. Everyone was on their feet screaming for their favorite driver, and even Dad was standing up, transfixed by the drama of the moment.

The finish was a bit of an anticlimax. With six laps to go, Baker's engine let go on the back straight in a huge cloud of smoke. Richard Petty coasted to victory two laps ahead of Bobby Isaac, who finished second. Thankfully. I'm not sure how much more even a thirteen-year-old's heart could have taken that afternoon. My very first stock-car race I got to watch my hero win, while I was jumping up and down in my seat cheering wildly. As he took his victory lap, Richard was once again smiling and waving at the crowd, and of course to the kid in the third row. I was certain he was looking right at me, the only race fan from Pennsylvania, as he drove by.

Before the Victory Lane ceremonies finished, the drizzle began falling again. It did seem indeed that Bill France had some sort of deal after all. The entire ride home, between swipes of the windshield, I was chattering away, "Did you see when . . . ," or "Remember when . . . ," at Dad over the noise of the engine. And he was smiling. Dad enjoyed the race after all, but more importantly he'd later tell me, I had enjoyed it more than he could have imagined, and that made the trials of getting there worthwhile.

Dad did not become a huge NASCAR fan, but after 1973, when the races came on he'd lay aside the *Times* and watch with me. In '79 when CBS began broadcasting the Daytona 500 live, we'd always watch it together, and I remember Dad actually pumping a fist in '79, willing Richard to get his engine refired and beat Pearson to the line, while I was going nuts on the sofa.

While Richard Petty is still involved with the sport as a team owner, neither he nor any of the other drivers who raced in the '73 500 still compete. Dad passed away some thirteen years ago. We watched part of the Bristol spring race in his hospital room the last Sunday of his life.

To all you fathers reading this who might have a son who has a passion for racing, may I suggest you watch the race with him this Father's Day and maybe ask a few questions? You'll see that what's chaos to an untrained eye is actually an art form. To any sons whose father might be a race fan, while you can't quite understand what the fuss is all about, why not sit down with Dad and try to figure out what everyone's raving about? It won't be hard to see. And to you fathers and sons who share an interest in the sport, enjoy it together this Father's Day. Because even if you are thirteen, and you think spending an afternoon with Dad when you could be with your friends is hopelessly lame, there's a day coming down the road when you'll wish you two had spent more time together while you could.

Trust me.

Matt McLaughlin

Now, That's What I Call Excited!

Victory Lane at a NASCAR race is one place where you just can't seem to get too excited. Or can you?

The NASCAR Winston Cup Series had made its way back home again for the 1990 October Charlotte race.

Many people refer to Charlotte as "home base" for the series because the majority of the race shops are within a fifty-mile radius of the city. Given that the bulk of the race teams are based in the area, most drivers and their team members choose to live nearby as well.

Davey and I decided because of the number of friends and family wanting to attend the race, we would rent a condominium at the Speedway to house everyone on race day. It was decided that while Davey raced, I would play hostess for the afternoon.

I picked out my clothes that morning while Davey gave me the watchful eye. I had chosen to wear a skirt and heeled shoes since I would most likely not be visiting the busy garage area inside the facility. Davey was not sure of my choice of clothing, reminding me of the long day ahead and that maybe, just maybe, I was getting "a little overdressed."

As fate would have it, Davey ran well all day; he took the lead numerous times and went on to win the race.

I grabbed our daughter, Krista (who was only ten months old at the time), to quickly drive around to Victory Lane in hopes of being there when Davey climbed out of the car to help him celebrate his big win.

As Krista and I approached, I noticed the celebration was already under way. It was at this time that I also realized things were maybe a bit scary for an infant, seeing that people were yelling and cameras were flashing. I was just not prepared for her outburst as the champagne started to fly.

Krista went into a wailing, crying fit like I had never seen from her before. I knew I must get her away from the chaos quickly, before she fell apart.

I very graciously (or so I thought) stepped back out of the line of fire to remove the two of us from the celebration. The camera crews had already encircled the Victory Lane area. My only choice was to step over a row of heavily manicured bushes.

As I stepped over the bushes (with Krista held tightly in my arms), lo and behold, the heel to my shoe caught the hem of my skirt.

Faster than lightning, my skirt was down around my ankles.

I had never been more mortified than I was at that very moment. As if things were not bad enough, a security guard (in his gentlemanly way) had to help pull my skirt back up for me, seeing that my hands were full with Krista.

I quietly thanked him and, with a burning red face, slipped out of the Victory Lane area and back into my car and sped as fast as I could back to our condo, hoping that perhaps the nice security guard was the only set of eyes that caught my ordeal. No such luck!

On my way back to the condo, I decided not to tell Davey of my mishap, for fear that he would be equally mortified.

When Davey returned later that afternoon, he asked me where I ran off to. He said, "I turned around, and you were gone."

I told him that Krista was a bit fussy, and I felt it best to put her down for a short nap.

Being the ever-so-witty person that he was, he said, "You know, I don't think I have ever seen you so excited. I have heard of kicking up your heels, but not dropping your skirt."

Davey used to joke that he had eyes in the back of his head. For just a moment, I believed him.

Liz Allison

$\overline{\underline{2}}$

UP TO SPEED

It's all about going around that little circle just a little bit faster.

Ken Schrader

A Champion All Around

*Why did I take up racing? Well, I was too lazy
to work and too chicken to steal.*

Kyle Petty

The date was November 19, 1978. The grandstands at
the two-and-a-half-mile Ontario Motor Speedway in
Ontario, California, were packed with race fans buzzing
with excitement. The running of the Los Angeles Times
500 Grand National (now NASCAR Winston Cup) race
was about to begin. Racing legend Richard Petty, who
had literally dominated NASCAR for many years in his
distinctive "Petty Blue and Red" #43 STP Dodge racing
machine, was eager for the start.

His opponents? Other hard-charging and hungry competitors like Cale Yarborough, Bobby Allison and David
Pearson. It would be an intense five-hundred-mile battle
for the win, and this was the only major track where victory had steadily eluded this lanky southern-spoken
champion from Randleman, N.C., the only major track in
Petty's career to tame his winning spirit.

Despite his six national championships earned through 1975, Petty's fortunes had slightly seemed to wane. In the Los Angeles Times 500 in 1977, he had set the track record of 154.905 mph, but victory had evaded him in that contest. Since finishing first in the Firecracker 400 in July of 1977, he had won only one pole—at North Wilkesboro Speedway in October that year. A win here would truly add another cherished track title to his remarkable career.

On Friday, November 17, Cale Yarborough, who had already won ten feature events in 1978, captured the desired pole position, his eighth of the season. He powered his First National Travelers Checks Olds to a record-setting speed of 156.190 miles per hour. Bobby Allison was hot on Cale's heels in his Bud Moore-prepared Norris Industries 1978 T-Bird, taking second spot. They had both eclipsed Petty's standing track record. But, qualified solidly in third place, Petty was confident he was still in the hunt.

That Sunday, as the battle cry "Gentlemen, start your engines!" rang out over the crowd, forty engines roared to life. Again, determined to win this time, Petty, now driving a Chevrolet, charged into the lead on lap 3, held it for two laps, Lennie Pond passed him and Petty took it back. Off and on, in the heat of the battle, Petty would charge his STP mount back into the lead, often battling valiantly against Bobby Allison, both swapping leads and driving their hardest to claim the Los Angeles Times 500 winner's trophy. The winning payoff would be great, but Petty wanted this victory even more for his record books.

Suddenly, on the front straight of the eighty-third lap, his engine failed. He was out of the race. Despite leading for thirty laps, he had still not conquered this ultra-modern California superspeedway. For one more extremely frustrating time, a victory there had just been snatched away through a sudden mechanical failure.

At that race, I was assigned to interview Petty, win or lose, for Mutual Radio Network. As he pulled off the track, I hurriedly grabbed my mike and tape recorder. Glancing down from the pressroom, I watched The King pull himself through his car window; sadness etched his face. I rushed down the elevator from the pressroom, but he was already ahead of me, head and shoulders down, his lengthy stride carrying him toward his transporter in the garage area.

As I hustled along some distance behind him, I pondered, *Should I yell out and stop him for my interview, or should I wait?* Each time I'd needed an interview in the past, he had given me a great one. I glanced at my watch. My three-hour time delay to the East Coast was not closing in yet. I decided to wait.

Head still down, Petty hurried to his transporter, clambered in and closed the door behind him. I came to a halt just outside his door. *I know this race meant a lot to him,* I thought to myself, *but I've never seen him look so down. I'll wait ten minutes, let him gain his composure and then knock on his door to get my interview.*

Miraculously, just five minutes later, his transporter door opened, and from it emerged an entirely different Richard Petty: The King, and the man that fans knew and loved. Dressed in his typical Western-style attire, a sharp ten-gallon hat perched on his head, smiling that hundred-karat Richard Petty smile.

I was almost speechless. Here was a six-time champion, completely out of a very important race in his career, and he had just emerged tall, erect and beaming from ear to ear as if he had just won!

Seeing me waiting with mike in hand, he approached me and said, "Kay, I guess you need me for another interview; how much time do you need?" My usual ten minutes, I told him, and I got every minute needed of those ten—an informative, complete interview. The network would love it.

As I dashed off to feed my broadcast to Mutual, I saw him stroll over to the chain-link fence, where a huge chorus of young fans was clamoring and yelling for his autograph. They didn't care that the race was still on; they wanted an autograph from The King himself, and he was glad to oblige.

Still shaking my head in wonder at his instant transformation, I rushed up to the pressroom, fed my interview to the network and completed my other assignments, then headed back to the garage. Forty minutes had elapsed, but to my amazement, with the race still blazing away in full progress, there was Richard Petty, still flashing that brilliant smile and signing autographs for everyone in sight. The line never stopped forming.

One young boy, not having a cap, program or jacket to get signed, ingeniously ran into the men's room, emerged with a sheet of paper towel and thrust it through the fence for his racing hero to sign. Minutes later, he walked away with a satisfied grin. That young man now had The King's treasured autograph.

In curiosity, I stayed and watched.

Petty never left that fence until every fan, young and old, had received his autograph, written in his own distinctive, flourishing style. He must have signed for at least an hour or more.

You see, Richard Petty has never let his fans down, no matter if he won or if he lost. He is living proof of what a true champion is all about, both on and off the racetrack.

That's one of the many reasons that he is rightfully called The King.

Kay Presto

An Unexpected Alliance

*An athlete is not crowned unless he competes
according to the rules.*

2 Timothy 2:5

The atmosphere was electric in Atlanta. Three NASCAR
drivers (Mark Martin, Dale Jarrett and Jeff Gordon) had
the chance to win the NASCAR Winston Cup championship in the last race of the season. The "hype" was extra-
ordinary all weekend, as seldom in the history of racing
have three people been in the position to win a championship with only one race left in the season. The championship is the highest achievement for any driver for the
entire year. It certainly was a momentous occasion for
these three men. It was a special weekend for thousands
of NASCAR fans.

During the day on Saturday, as these drivers were
hounded by the media for stories, the most remarkable
story was forming quietly between those three drivers
and me. A special meeting was being planned that would
occur following the usual Saturday Bible study that met

in Mark's motor coach in the infield area reserved for the drivers and owners.

Shortly after 7:30 P.M., everyone left the study except Mark, Dale, Jeff and me. What was about to happen probably had never happened in the history of racing. In fact, it probably had not happened in any major sport on the eve of a championship game. Seldom would any professional athlete commune with their opponents in any kind of setting. But here in the quietness of Mark Martin's motor coach, this unique experience was unfolding.

After we chatted a moment, Mark Martin, unquestionably one of the toughest race-car drivers ever; Dale Jarrett, who came from a racing pedigree; and Jeff Gordon, loved and hated for the absolute dominance he brought to racing, joined me in holding hands for a special time of prayer. Dale started the prayer, asking God for safety and to give Mark and Jeff a good day of racing that would be fun and exciting. Mark prayed, expressing thanks for allowing him to be in the position for the championship with these drivers, and for God's graciousness for giving him the privilege to race. Jeff began to communicate his gratitude to God and how much God meant to him, and asked that God would allow each of the drivers to be at their best and not have any difficulties during the race. They were united in their prayers—"We give this race to you, God."

Max Helton

Reprinted by permission of Mike Smith, Las Vegas Sun.

Sometimes Success Takes Time

I think growing up around the sport of stock-car racing, I always knew that's the business I'd end up spending my life around. Did I think the sport would end up as big as it is now, or that it would provide the kind of life that it has for my family and myself? Not really. I just knew I enjoyed watching racing and being around it as a kid, and if I could make a living doing something I love, then why not.

The world of NASCAR Winston Cup racing has changed considerably since I was a child, watching guys like my dad, Richard Petty and David Pearson compete. Growing up in the shadow of a champion can be a daunting task. I'm very proud of what my dad accomplished both on the racetrack and off. He set quite an example, both as a competitor and human being. Even today, everywhere I go, people constantly ask about my dad and tell me what a gentleman he is. It makes me very proud to be a Jarrett.

Despite growing up the son of a racing champion, creating a career in racing was not an easy job. I'm not one of these guys who started racing at the age of five and just progressively moved from series to series. Those opportunities weren't as available when I was a kid as they are today. So, I diverted my interest in competition to high-school sports. I kept busy with football, basketball, baseball and golf. I enjoyed the competition aspect of those sports and put 110 percent into those activities. It even paid off to the extent that I was offered a couple of football scholarships to some small colleges. I was even offered a golf scholarship to the University of South Carolina. I was so into golf that if you asked my dad, he really thought I would be on the PGA Tour today rather than the NASCAR Winston Cup Series tour.

I got married right out of high school and quickly became a dad to my oldest son Jason. Being married with a child at eighteen required a job. At that time, my dad owned our local racetrack—Hickory Motor Speedway. He was gracious enough to give me a job there, and that's probably where I decided that I really wanted to have a career in racing.

Like I said earlier, my path to the NASCAR Winston Cup Series wasn't nearly as conventional as that of many of the guys who compete today. While holding down a regular job, I'd spend my evenings with a couple of my high-school buddies who were also interested in racing. Andy Petree, who is now a NASCAR Winston Cup car owner, and Jimmy Newsome were those two friends. The three of us actually built the first car I ever raced. In my first race I started twenty-fifth and finished ninth. From then on, my mind was made up that racing was what I had to do.

It hasn't been easy, but sitting here today, I can tell you that everything has worked out the way it was supposed to.

After my first marriage ended in divorce, I focused every waking minute on my racing career. I started competing in the Limited Sportsman Division at Hickory Motor Speedway. While competing at Hickory and working to support my racing career, I met my wife Kelley. We had both grown up around Hickory, and we knew it was where we wanted to live our lives and raise a family. We married and started to build our life together. It wasn't easy in the early days, and a lot of times we were almost broke just trying to build my racing career. Kelley was a teacher, and we know they are well underpaid for all they do.

In the early 1980s, I started competing in a series that eventually became what is now called the NASCAR Busch Series. It was at this time that I started getting the attention of some of the car owners in the NASCAR Winston Cup Series. I competed in a few Cup races here and there during the mid-1980s. In 1988, I competed in twenty-nine races with four different car owners.

I finally got the break of my career in 1990. It didn't come until after the 1990 NASCAR Winston Cup Series season had already started. I got a call from the Wood Brothers. Neil Bonnett had started the '90 season driving their #21 Ford, but was involved in a crash at Darlington that prevented him from competing the rest of the season. I didn't have a ride at the time and I really wasn't sure what was going to happen. They asked me to step in and drive, and it ended up becoming a full-time job. To this day, I tell everyone that if it hadn't been for Len and Eddie Wood, I might not have made it as a NASCAR Winston Cup Series driver. Not only did the Wood Brothers give me a career boost, they also gave me their friendship. Eddie Wood is still one of my closest friends. I scored my first NASCAR Winston Cup victory at Michigan in 1991 and was thrilled to be able to put the Wood Brothers Ford back in the victory lane. It was a wonderful way to help repay them for believing in me and giving me such a great opportunity.

I have been very fortunate throughout my NASCAR Winston Cup racing career. I've won some of NASCAR's biggest races, such as the Daytona 500 and the Brickyard 400. In addition to the Wood Brothers, I have been able to compete for two gentlemen who will go down in history as NASCAR's most successful and respected car owners, Joe Gibbs and Robert Yates. I was able to give Robert Yates his first NASCAR Winston Cup championship when we won that title in 1999. I hope to be able to win that second championship for Robert Yates before the time comes to hang up my helmet.

It's kind of funny how my life and career have taken shape. I always tell people that Jeff Gordon and I have been racing the same amount of years. The only difference is he started when he was five years old, and I started when I was twenty! Although my racing career has been a struggle at times, it has also been very gratifying. It has taken place one slow step at a time. I've always been a believer that things are brought to you when you can handle them. Remember, good things come to those who wait.

I am in the midst of what has been a very rewarding career. I am able to make a living at something I love to do. It has provided for my family and me in ways I never dreamed possible. I'm able to provide a wonderful life for my wife, Kelley, and our three kids, Natalee, Karsyn and Zachary. Most of my favorite moments are spent at home with Kelley watching the kids play basketball and soccer. I also enjoy the times I am able to watch my oldest son, Jason, race in the ARCA Series. I'm pretty proud of the fact that one of the traits I have passed on to my children is their competitive nature.

A lot of times my career keeps me away from home with testing, sponsor commitments and races. I am always amazed at how Kelley juggles her job of taking care of our kids, keeping up with their schedules, keeping me informed on how well they are doing and then making it to as many races as possible. She is truly an amazing person.

For now the Jarrett family is going to keep on competing. Now that I'm getting older, the question I get asked a lot is whether I've thought about retirement. I always tell people that I have to keep racing because our youngest son, Zach, is just eight years old, and I've still got to put him, Natalee and Karsyn through college. That's true, but I also plan to keep on racing until I feel I can't be competitive anymore. I love my job, and I thank God every day when I wake up that I get to do what I love doing for a living. I know how fortunate I am to be able to do that. It hasn't always been an easy way of life, but racing has been good to the Jarrett family for many years, and I hope it continues to be that way for many years to come. More importantly, I hope that the Jarrett family has been and continues to be good for the sport of NASCAR racing.

Dale Jarrett

Racing School on a Budget

The best way to make a small fortune in racing is to start with a big one.

Junior Johnson

I've always wanted to attend one of those racing schools like Fast Track, The Richard Petty Driving Experience or maybe even the Skip Barber driving school. I can just imagine myself barreling through the turns in a finely tuned racing machine, the sound of the yowling engine and barking tires transporting me into fits of epiphany. While the world blurs by in a wash of speed, I also take in the smell of burning rubber, high-octane fuel and the acrid smell of my instructor dampening his fire-retardant suit.

However, silly things like not having any money have always hampered my dream. I've appealed to my wife to let me go and sell a kidney, but she always forbids me from doing it. Her reasoning is that I shouldn't be selling any kidneys on account of she might need one of them one day, and that she would hate to leave me without any kidneys at all. Even if I could sell a kidney, chances are it would only get me halfway. I might even be able to afford one of those "discount" driving experiences that lets you actually lean in and *smell* the interior of a real race car. *Sigh.* Just as I had given up on my dream, I discovered an affordable alternative that had been there all along. Nestled in the foothills of Jasper, Alabama, not ten miles from my own home, lies Sonny's Fast Track, a veritable haven for the aspiring racer on a budget. Instead of costing several thousand dollars, you pay just five dollars for five minutes in one of their professionally prepared racers. Sounded like a good deal to me, so I grabbed my son and a twenty-dollar bill and we headed off to Sonny's.

My son Isaac is only seven, but I have raised the boy to race. I started sitting him down in front of Playstation when he could do little more than drool on the controller and goggle at nothing in particular. We worked our way through numerous driving games such as Grand Turismo, and both Driver and Driver 2. In the beginning, I would have to stop and wait on him while he figured how to bite on the controller to make the little on-screen racer go. Now, almost seven years later, he routinely whoops my tail on every driving game in our library. The boy was ready for the real thing.

Once at the track, we paid for four tickets and got a fifth one free. Surprisingly, there was no one else at the track, and our driving instructor was nowhere to be found. I went back to the booth where we bought our tickets and asked where our instructor might be. I was told that he was "behind the shed, whackin' them weeds." I followed the sound of the weed trimmer and found not a seasoned racing instructor, but a surly sixteen-year-old wearing a Korn T-shirt.

Mr. Surly tried his best not to roll his eyes when I told him what I wanted, but ending up losing that battle. After dropping the weed trimmer carelessly to the ground, he started shuffling toward the racetrack with slightly more enthusiasm than an ornery tomcat being stuffed into a pet taxi.

Mr. Surly opened the gate to the track, and my son and I both caught our breath—before us was a five-turn road course laid out on an expanse almost big enough for a miniature golf course. To our right, the racing machines sat silent, waiting for a hungry driver to take the helm. My son immediately chose the replica of the #28 Havoline car, and I chose the #43 STP.

In less than four nanoseconds, Isaac was belted in and ready to rumble, whereas I was still trying to figure out how to get in the damn thing. I see now why 6'5" Michael Waltrip is such an advocate for the taller greenhouse in WC cars. Finally, I decided the best way to get in this beast was to straddle it, then fold all 6'3" of me into a compartment that looked no bigger than a Buster Brown shoebox. Okay ... Ah! I was in, or at least my tail-end was, because my feet were still sticking out either side. Once I got my right leg in so I could operate the pedals, I found that I could no longer turn the steering wheel to the right because my knee was jammed against it. After deciding my left knee would not fit in my ear, I decided to leave my other leg dangling out in front of the car. I'm glad I couldn't see myself. I've never had a desire to know what a rhinoceros sitting on a skateboard looked like. But hey, I was in the car, and that was what mattered.

Mr. Surly pushed both of our cars out onto the track, and I began looking for the series of ignition switches like I've seen on television. Then I saw Mr. Surly walk to the rear of Isaac's car and pull a rope several times, and I heard a powerful motor mutter to life. He came around to my car and did the same, then told me that (I am not making this up!) the pedal on the right side made it go, and the one on the left made it stop. Humph! Some instructor he turned out to be. I gassed it and pulled even with Isaac. We exchanged a look, and our first real race against one another was on.

We went into the first turn, a left-hander, side by side, and when I got on the brakes and cut the wheel to enter the turn, nothing happened. I kept on going straight as my son whipped through the first turn, his triumphant laughter just barely reaching my ears over the engine noise and the sound of skidding tires. Just as I was about to tag the wall, the #43 machine finally cooperated and entered the turn. The machine behaved the exact same way with the four other turns as well, and the right turns were especially difficult, seeing as how I could not turn the wheel in that direction without risking serious kneecap damage. As I came around to the start/finish line, I tried yelling out to our instructor that I had developed a bad push, but he was too busy drinking a Mountain Dew and tugging on the seat of his pants.

Halfway through our third lap, I began to hear something behind me. Daring a look over my shoulder, I saw Isaac closing in on my rear bumper. The shame! The embarrassment! After all I had taught him, after all the times I waited for him to catch up with me on Playstation games, my own son was about to put me a lap down! As if this was not bad enough, he made hard contact going into the next turn and sent me tail first into the tire barrier. My only consolation in this was seeing Isaac slam into the wall on the next turn because he was laughing so hard.

We both got going again, but I never got close to him until he came around to lap me the second time. I was spared that indignity when the "last lap" flasher went off. Apparently Mr. Surly, who had finished his Mountain Dew and successfully extracted the seat of his pants from the nether regions, realized that we had exceeded our seat time and called us in. I pulled into my space, gently nudging the tire barrier before coming to a complete stop. Isaac pulled in next, slamming the barrier hard enough to send a tire flying over his head and send Mr. Surly ducking for cover.

"I won, didn't I?" Isaac asked, grinning like a fiend.

"I think you won several times, Isaac," I said. His grin broadened, and he said two absolutely crushing words to me, words that I will never forget, words that I will never let *him* forget.

"You're slow." Translation: You're old.

"I'll get you next time, you little cuss," I said. Yeah, right. Unless I drop fifty pounds, shrink six inches and lose about four shoe sizes, I'll never get in one of these things again. I didn't even know if I'd be getting *out* of this one.

I was able to get out without the Jaws of Life. I do not wish to speak much of this experience, but let me say that it did involve doing a handstand at one point. My doctor says the cast can come off in just a few more months, and that is very encouraging.

We still had three tickets to ride left between us, and I let Isaac run without me. I leaned on the outside gate watching him go. He never ran as fast by himself as he did when I was on the track. Without me out there to beat, he was just out there having fun, bumping into things on purpose, laughing like a loon, weaving back and forth like he's seen the NASCAR Winston Cup guys do during a caution. I tried to yell at him that his tires were already warm and he was just scrubbing off speed, but he didn't hear me. Not that he would have listened anyway.

Well, I'd had my driving-school experience. Not quite what I had in mind, and I didn't really learn anything, except that giving my son the chance to beat his ol' dad in a race for real was worth every penny.

Steve Wingate

I'm Alive

I grew up racing motorcycles in Southern California. I got so beat up that my parents wouldn't let me race bikes anymore. My mom couldn't stand watching me race as a kid because she was afraid I would get hurt. My dad loved racing; he loved the battle. But if I fell, that's where he had the problem. My dad could not stand being in the hospital—being wherever I was—if I was injured. That's where my mom would step in. I had reconstructive knee surgery when I was eight years old, and they had to totally rebuild my knee. When they popped the X rays on the machine in front of the light, my dad passed out. They brought in another stretcher to put him on.

My parents were both watching the crash that afternoon of June 25, 2000. It was the NASCAR Busch Series race at Watkins Glen, and we had an awesome day going. I was really looking forward to the road-course race, and we were sticking to our plan on fuel strategy. We came out of the pits and had completed only one lap when it happened.

The brakes failed. I was looking underneath the lapped car. I got on the brake pedal, and the brake pedal went to the floor. I knew I only had one move. I thought about running into the back of the car in front of me, but I was going so fast. I thought, *Man, I'm not going to hurt him as well.* So, I turned to the right trying to get into the inside wall, but as soon as I got into the infield grass, the car went straight again and bounced around and left the racetrack.

I was airborne and cleared the sand trap. In the air, I thought, *Man, this is really going to be bad.* I was expecting it to be concrete and, when I was in the air, I just lowered my head down to my chest, so I wouldn't get whiplash. I pulled my feet back and relaxed my body as much as I could so I would be limber when I hit.

I saw a deal on television that I'm sure everybody has seen with Rusty Wallace, Kenny Schrader and a whole bunch of different guys talking about their big crashes. Every one of them talks about how they lowered their head and relaxed themselves for the crash.

I don't know what inside of me remembered that show when I was doing 140 miles per hour about ready to crash. One thing that worked for me is that I knew there was nothing I could do. I was in trouble, and there was this calming attitude. It was like, "Okay, here it comes and it's going to be big. . . . Be ready." I just tried to stay relaxed, closed my eyes and put my life in the Lord's hands. I knew my parents, my family, my girlfriend and friends were watching, and I really thought they'd be taking me out of there unconscious.

Then I hit the wall. The car was on fire, and I was sitting in a pile of thermal foam thinking, *Oh man, my legs are okay, my body is all right, my arms work.*

I put my window net down, and the fans went crazy. When I got out of the car, they were jumping up and down with their arms in the air, and this adrenaline rush came over me.

Next thing you know, I was on the roof of the car. I had my arms up in the air just thankful that God was riding with me on that one. It was like a victory salute on top of the car, and I was thinking, *I'm alive!*

Jimmie Johnson
As told to Claire B. Lang

A NASCAR® Racing Night

Jim Inglebright was eager to do well at this race. Sponsored only by himself, his #20 NASCAR Featherlite Southwest Tour Series car bore his company's name, "Road Runner Towing." It was 1993. Jim was a rookie in the series, but he felt he could be lucky in the event. It was also his twelfth wedding anniversary. His wife Valerie, mom Judy, and adored little girl Jordan had come to see him compete.

As he waited his turn to qualify, a track official ran over to his car. "Come quick!" he yelled to Inglebright. "Your little girl just fell off the grandstand." Jim's feeling of luck turned to panic. Unbuckling and climbing out of his car, he could only envision Jordan with a fractured skull and broken arms and legs. Those grandstands were twenty feet high.

He rushed over to her. The paramedics were already checking Jordan for signs of injury. A tiny three-year-old, she had slipped through the space at the top of the grandstand, hit the cross-bracing as she fell and landed flat on her back. Three men had seen her fall and had leaped over the fence to her aid.

As Jim approached her, Jordan was crying. With the paramedics' okay, he cradled her in his arms. Her crying stopped. Finding no injuries, they allowed Inglebright to carry her to his transporter. A track official hurried over. "Because of Jordan's accident, we've let you qualify last. You have to go now!"

Racing back to his car, he climbed in, buckled up and donned his helmet. His engine roared to life, and #20 rolled out onto the three-eighths-of-a-mile oval. But Jim's mind was not on qualifying—it was on Jordan. "I have to get back to her," he kept saying, as he picked up speed and circled the track.

When he finished his run, a roar went up from the crowd. He had set a new qualifying lap record at the track—14.343 seconds—which still stands today (April 2003).

Dashing out of his car, Inglebright rushed over to his transporter. A doctor had checked Jordan over completely and found that, remarkably, she had no injuries at all. Was it the soft ground that protected Jordan? The cross-bracing that broke her fall on the way down? No one could really say for sure.

All Jim knew was that he was eternally grateful. Climbing back into his car, he not only raced hard that night, but he won the main event, outrunning such stars as Doug George and Ron Hornaday. To this day, he often can't remember which driver he beat to the stripe that night because his concentration was so focused on Jordan.

It had been an evening that started out with joy, terror, and then joy. "It was our anniversary, then Jordan escaped injury and then I won that race as a rookie, against the toughest in that sport," Inglebright recalled.

Did they go out to celebrate? In a way, they did. According to Jim, they went straight home to celebrate that everything that evening had turned out so incredibly well.

Kay Presto

[AUTHOR'S NOTE: *At the time Jim told this story, Jordan had grown to be a lively, healthy twelve-year-old.*]

READER/CUSTOMER CARE SURVEY

CC8

We care about your opinions. Please take a moment to fill out this Reader Survey card and mail it back to us.
As a special **"thank you"** we'll send you exciting news about interesting books and a valuable **Gift Certificate.**

Please PRINT using ALL CAPS

First Name | MI. | Last Name

Address

City | ST | Zip

Phone # ( ) - | Fax # ( ) -

Email

(1) Gender:
____ Female ____ Male

(2) Age:
____ 12 or under ____ 40-59
____ 13-19 ____ 60+
____ 20-39

(3) Marital Status
____ Married
____ Single
____ Divorced/Widowed

(4) Did you receive this book as a gift?
____ Yes ____ No

(5) How many Chicken Soup books have you bought or read?
____ 1 ____ 2-4 ____ 5+

(6) How did you find out about this book?
Please fill in ONE.
1) ____ Recommendation
2) ____ Store Display
3) ____ Bestseller List
4) ____ Online
5) ____ Advertisement
6) ____ Catalog/Mailing
7) ____ Interview/Review (TV, Radio, Print)

(7) Where do you usually buy books?
Please fill in your top TWO choices.
1) ____ Bookstore
2) ____ Religious Bookstore
3) ____ Online
4) ____ Book Club/Mail Order
5) ____ Price Club (Costco, Sam's Club, etc.)
6) ____ Retail Store (Target, Wal-Mart, etc.)

(9) What subjects do you enjoy reading about most? Rank only *FIVE*. Use 1 for your favorite, 2 for second favorite, etc.

	1	2	3	4	5
1) Parenting/Family	○	○	○	○	○
2) Relationships	○	○	○	○	○
3) Recovery/Addictions	○	○	○	○	○
4) Health/Nutrition	○	○	○	○	○
5) Christianity	○	○	○	○	○
6) Spirituality/Inspiration	○	○	○	○	○
7) Business Self-Help	○	○	○	○	○
8) Teen Issues	○	○	○	○	○
9) Sports	○	○	○	○	○

(14) What attracts you most to a book?
(Please rank 1-4 in order of preference.)

	1	2	3	4
14) Title	○	○	○	○
15) Cover Design	○	○	○	○
16) Author	○	○	○	○
17) Content	○	○	○	○

TAPE IN MIDDLE; DO NOT STAPLE

BUSINESS REPLY MAIL

FIRST-CLASS MAIL PERMIT NO 45 DEERFIELD BEACH, FL

POSTAGE WILL BE PAID BY ADDRESSEE

CHICKEN SOUP FOR THE SOUL OF NASCAR
HEALTH COMMUNICATIONS, INC.
3201 SW 15TH STREET
DEERFIELD BEACH FL 33442-9875

IııIIıııIIıılıılıIıılıılıIIIıIıılıılıIııılılıılıIıl

FOLD HERE

Comments:

Do you have your own Chicken Soup story that you would like to send us? Please submit separately to: Chicken Soup for the Soul, P.O. Box 30880, Santa Barbara, CA 93130

Look Who's Following

If you don't know where you're going, how will you get there?

Casey Stengel

My mom and dad raised my brother, sister and me with faith. My dad, Ned Jarrett—also a NASCAR champion—was racing sixty to seventy times a year, so we were on the road a lot. When we were home, we attended church as much as possible. When we were on the road, the Christian values instilled in us didn't change.

My dad is a very driven person. He wanted to succeed and be the best at whatever he was doing, whether it was in the race car or as the promoter of our local racetrack after he retired from driving. He had the best short track going at the time, and when he got into broadcasting, he worked hard to be the best at that, too . . . but he didn't do it in a way that he was stepping over people.

He had everyone's best interest at heart, whether it was his family or someone in the business. He's a good example of how you can be very successful without being ruthless, as we often see in business today.

At the time my dad was driving, there were a lot of shady dealings going on at the track. But Dad believed if he worked harder and used the strengths that he had, it would benefit him more. He has always had a very strong faith in the Lord and felt it would carry him a lot farther than the other things that were going on at that time.

I do a lot of listening and praying to God, too. I have certainly been blessed in many, many ways—not only on the racetrack, but also with my entire family.

In '95, I was driving the Texaco car for Robert Yates. That was a one-year deal, and I knew it was going to be up. Ernie Irvan was coming back to drive the car the next year. My reason for going to Robert's in the first place, leaving the great situation that I had at Joe Gibbs's operation, was for the opportunity to own my own team. I had owned my own Busch team for a number of years, and I felt I could have a successful NASCAR Winston Cup team if I could find adequate sponsorship. Robert had agreed to help me, but it didn't quite work out that way.

I was in the final negotiations on a sponsorship proposal from Hooters Restaurants. I could have my own team. I was in the process of putting everything together and had just met with the people from Hooters. The money they offered was a little shy of what I needed, but they had assured me they would help me secure an associate sponsorship. Robert Yates had agreed to provide my engines, so we were pretty much on our way.

Later on, as my wife and I discussed it, we decided that it just wasn't the best situation for me, as far as the image I tried to project. There is nothing wrong with the food at Hooters or its atmosphere; it just wasn't something that I felt completely comfortable with. I began to think that trying to raise a family while having to make thirty appearances at Hooters might not be the best situation. By making promotional appearances at that type of place,

I felt it would be difficult for the majority of Christians out there to take my testimony seriously. So we prayed for something else to come along, and it did. Before I signed that contract with Hooters on the Wednesday before Bristol, Robert Yates came to me and asked if I would be interested in driving a Ford-sponsored car for the second team he was starting. Things do work in a hurry if you talk to the Lord about them! After a lot of soul-searching and praying, the answer was there. It was easy for me to make that decision.

I was happy with what was going on at Robert Yates Racing and certainly in making the right decision. It was the best thing for me and my family. Since then, we've won a championship and a lot of races. It proves that if you listen and follow what God has to tell you, you are going to be rewarded.

I remembered a story my dad once told me about how our actions can affect others. One day he was racing on a dirt track and quickly realized during practice that once the race started, if he was going to be successful, he would have to pick certain objects above the dust to serve as markers. Then when he saw the markers, he'd know it was time to turn.

Sure enough, soon after the race started, the dust built up quickly. He couldn't even see the car in front of him, but Dad was prepared. He began looking for his markers, and it worked. Lap after lap, he navigated the track, using the markers as his guide.

All was going well until he was driving hard down the backstretch into turn three. He couldn't see his marker, but he knew something was coming up soon. All of a sudden, the track got real bumpy. It was obvious something wasn't right. Once the dust cleared, he realized the car he was using as a marker in turn three was gone, and he was in the parking lot!

It was quite a sight, but what made it even more interesting was that a group of other race cars was right behind him! Now, Dad realized why he was sitting in the parking lot, but he got out to ask the other drivers why they were there. They simply said, "You're the champion. We couldn't see anything either, so we've been following you!"

Dale Jarrett with Max Helton and Ron Camacho

3

THE WORLD'S GREATEST FANS

If it weren't for the fans, we wouldn't be out there in the first place doing what we love to do. Every time I sign an autograph, it's like saying thank you to the fans for letting me do what I love to do, and make a living out of it.

Richard Petty

"For the next few months, you're going to have to be the man of the house. Be nice to your mother and sister. If you need me, I'll be in the den watching NASCAR."

Reprinted by permission of Mike Shapiro.

Why I Am a Race Fan

Do not speak evil of one another, brethren.

James 4:11

Ward Burton has offered to help a six-year-old boy he met at an autograph session, who was born with a cleft palate, and after meeting him, Ward has offered to pay for any surgery needed to correct his condition. Not only has Ward's kindness touched me, but it has reinforced something I've known about NASCAR—the drivers, the teams, etc.—for over thirty years now: By and large, this is the nicest group of athletes around.

We all know that stock-car racing got its start from "whiskey runners" in their souped-up cars, but you don't hear of the drivers being involved in betting scandals, drugs, fixing races, or any other illegal or unsavory activities. Look at the constant labor disputes in other organized sports. NASCAR drivers do get a salary annually, but most of their income is based on their performance. If they finish poorly, their pay reflects it. Talk about incentive! Sure, they make money from their endorsements, but their future is based on their track performance on race day.

We've all heard the athletes in other professional sports saying that they don't want to be role models. When was the last time you heard a driver saying that? Not only are the majority of them family men, but men of God as well. They seem to accept being a role model as part of their responsibility to the sport.

The next time you get mad at a driver because he did something you were not in favor of or took offense to on the track, stop to think: For every bad deed on the track, how many good deeds were done off the track?

I know who my heroes are, even though I may not be pulling for all of them on race day.

Mark Moore

A True NASCAR® Fan

It is not the size of a man but the size of his heart that matters.

Evander Holyfield

I am truly amazed at the pride NASCAR fans take in their drivers. They will defend them to the bitter end, right or wrong, black or white. I must admit, I am the same way. But when tragedy strikes this sport, fans rally around each other to offer strength and support. Several examples of this phenomenon can be seen by looking at the history of NASCAR, the 2001 season especially. This year offered a great example of how, time and time again, this sport finds the strength to pull together amidst terrible tragedy.

February 18, 2001, changed NASCAR racing as we knew it. It was one of the most exciting Daytona 500s in recent memory, as it produced some of the closest side-by-side racing we had seen in ages. In the closing laps, NASCAR officials had to be feeling like they were sitting on top of the world. The new television package was well on its way to making the sport even more successful than it had been in the past, and everything seemed to be going in their favor.

In the blink of an eye, everything changed. On the last lap in the last turn, the sport's biggest star was taken away. I will never forget the chill that ran down my spine when I heard Mike Helton's address to the media: "We've lost Dale Earnhardt." My heart sank to my feet, and the tears flowed fast and furious. The next images I remember seeing were the fans lining up to leave mementos and spend time with one another in an attempt to grieve and support each other, as well as offer their condolences to the family and the sport they love.

I remember getting calls the next day at work from patients who knew my driver of choice. It has never been difficult for people to figure out. I am the typical fan who has shirts, jackets, cups, key chains and just about every product imaginable with the signature #3. These people took time out of their busy schedules to call and let me know that their thoughts were with me and every other racing fan who grieved for the loss of their driver. It was very touching, but not unexpected, as NASCAR fans are some of the best people you will ever know.

Time passed and the schedule moved forward, albeit with an obvious strain on the sport. Soon enough it would be time for me to attend my first live event of the season at California Speedway. I looked forward to it, as I always do. Attending a live race is an experience beyond most others. And while I couldn't wait to be there, I also felt uneasiness, as it would be my first trip to the track for a race since Dale's passing. It was also to be his fiftieth birthday.

Before I knew it, I was sitting in the grandstands on April 29, 2001. And even though I had done some media work that morning, I knew I wanted to be among the fans for the event. Climbing the stairs to reach my seat, I wondered what would lie ahead and how emotional an event it would truly be. What took place would surpass my expectations of emotion and healing.

As the green flag fell, my heart began to sink, for it was finally hitting me that I was sitting in the stands for an event that my driver wouldn't be attending. The tears began to flow as the field approached lap 3, which was designated as a silent tribute to Dale Earnhardt for the remainder of the 2001 season.

As the field crossed the start/finish line to begin the third lap, I found three fingers held high in the air and tears streaming down my face. I looked to the fans in front of and behind me who carried much the same baggage as I. What really caught my eye was a very young girl who sat in the stands with her parents. She couldn't have been more than four years old, with blonde curly locks and a grin that could melt the heart of the sternest of men.

She held her three fingers high while a tear rolled down her cheek. It was clear she missed her champion. She was there to support his son as she cheered for him each and every lap, but it was clear to her that something was missing. Adorned in the apparel that supported her driver, she took her place among the 110,000 people who were there to take part in the event. And while race fans are very supportive of their sport and their driver, it was plainly clear that some folks were there to take part in the emotions of the moment and to pay tribute to one of the most heralded legends of all time.

The little girl slowly took her seat and, through her mourning, managed a smile for her mother and father. They patted her on the head, but it was clear—she was disturbed. As the laps clicked past, this young girl continued to cheer for the drivers, but every so often she would hold up her three fingers as a tear would roll down her cheek. In watching this young girl, I realized just how much this man was loved by his fans. This young girl was there to impress no one. Despite the fans who held their signs, jumping in and out of the camera's view in hopes of claiming their television air space, this young girl was there to pay tribute. She wanted to experience the healing that takes place among fans.

By the end of the day, the group around us shared emotion, happiness and, with Rusty Wallace's win, closure. Rusty paid tribute to his fallen friend by taking a victory lap waving the #3 flag from his driver's window. I looked down at the young girl, who was beaming with pride. There were no more tears. Rather, she was full of joy and happiness that her champion had been recognized.

It was then that I realized that by sitting in the stands that day, the healing had begun for all of us. The people around us marveled at that young girl's spirit. Her devotion and emotion were heartbreaking, yet offered us all healing as we could finally begin to celebrate the life of this champion.

To that young girl, wherever you may be, we all owe you a debt of thanks. Your innocence and dedication inspired us all.

Lori Tyler

Reprinted by permission of Mike Smith, Las Vegas Sun.

Running with the Big Guys

The good Lord doesn't tell you what his plans are, so all you can do is get up in the morning and see what happens next.

Richard Petty

Roaring engines, crowded bleachers and the stench of stale beer mingled with the reeking fumes of unburned hydrocarbons. What was I, fastidious soul that I am, doing in a place like this?

I was bringing Mike* to Talladega Superspeedway. Confined to a wheelchair, fifteen-year-old Mike was passionate as any kid can be about sports. He was here to add his voice to the noise of the crowd as he watched Davey Allison vie with Bill Elliott and Kyle Petty for yet another racing honor. Mike loved the roar of the engines, even if he would never know what it feels like to have that much engine power in his hands. His foot would never put the pedal to the metal.

This excursion was a once-in-a-lifetime treat for Mike. He was near the end of his fight with Duchenne's

*Name has been changed.

dystrophy and had no use of his arms and legs, but he did have a stout heart and as much courage as any of those guys down there in the pits.

If this weren't Talladega Day, Mike and I would be doing what we usually do on swell summer days: going for a walk, which was really a "roll" for Mike and a pretty good workout for me. Mike loved to go fast, with the rush of the wind in his face.

"C'mon, Lynne," he'd yell. "Just one more lap."

Racing down the road, I'd run as fast as I could, pushing Mike's wheelchair, the hot tar of the street sticking to the soles of my white nurse's shoes. We'd both laugh as his carrot-red hair flew in the wind we created.

Come NASCAR season, Sundays would find us camped in front of the television watching the big race. I'd make the popcorn and Mike would tediously feed himself, one kernel at a time, using three fingers of his right hand, the only limbs he could still move. More and more, I would feed him the kernels. One time I got caught up in the race and wasn't paying attention to him. I kept sticking popcorn in his mouth until finally, with bulging cheeks, he bit me to get my attention. I had off-tracked badly.

Mike never took the easy way. Rather than having auto magazines mailed to the house, he endured his journeys to the bookstore so he could survey his options. These trips were not simple affairs, but if Mike could bear the pain of the preparations, I could bear to help him. As I washed and dressed him on his bed, Mike occupied himself by looking at the faces that gazed down from his bedroom walls: life-sized posters of Kyle Petty and Cale Yarborough lovingly and intricately framed by his dad. Mike would peer at his heroes, drawing courage and endurance just by thinking about their feats and dream of slipstreaming at two hundred miles per hour. I'd smile to myself, aware that none of those strong, brave men had more heart than my Mike.

Once, as I waited in the bookstore while Mike browsed through car magazines, I noticed an old man watching us. Just as we were leaving the store, the fellow approached us and, without speaking, reached into the pocket of his work pants and then placed a wrinkled dollar bill on Mike's lap—a shy tribute to Mike's courage.

"Gee," Mike said, "I wish he hadn't done that."

"Ah, Mike," I said, "you've got a fan. The nicest thing you can do for someone is to let them be nice to you. I'll bet he feels pretty good right about now."

Shortly after our trip to Talladega, Mike finished his race. His last lap was an easy one. He went in his sleep to go run with the big guys. I gave the undertaker Mike's faded sweatshirt with the logo of his favorite hero, Kyle Petty. Later I placed pom-poms of carnations on his coffin, topped by a black-and-white checkered winner's flag, and said good-bye to the bravest kid I've ever known and my favorite athlete.

Lynne Zielinski

Simple Pleasures

As an adult, it's sometimes easy to become jaded about life and miss seeing the joy in small events. I think that's why God allows us to be parents. Living the joy that my ten-year-old feels about racing has softened my heart and given me new perspective.

Such was the case when we traveled to the inaugural race at Kansas City to see the NASCAR Busch and Winston Cup races. Though I'd been to races before, this was the first for my son, Colby, and he was thrilled to be at the first race of a new track, but even more thrilled with the lineup of plans I'd made. Not being much of a navigator, I seemed to get lost every time we went out. But rather than become frustrated, I was able to laugh that each time we did get lost, we happened upon another show car. We saw Jeff Gordon's car, my son's favorite, while looking for Wendy's to have lunch. We saw the Tide car ride simulator at a grocery store while driving ten miles out of our way looking for an interstate on-ramp. We chanced into seeing the M&M's car as it was being unloaded (what a thrill that sound is!) when we were lost in the same place on a different day (although I decided it didn't count as being lost since I'd been there before).

Our first night in town, I'd planned to go to a fan celebration at a local fairground where many drivers were scheduled to appear. Hoping for an autograph, we soon realized that the line had formed even before we arrived, and so we stood and waited. Our target this time was Rusty Wallace. The adult in me might have been leaning toward wondering how long this wait would be, but my son's joy and anticipation eclipsed any skepticism I might have otherwise felt. He would run from place to place taking picture after picture, and then report back to me, the designated line-stander.

His first (and maybe best) thrill came when Mark Martin was up on the stage talking to the people gathered. Ten-year-old Colby, seemingly without any inhibitions, walked up to the stage and stood just six feet from Mark Martin, pointing a camera in his direction. Not settling for one quick shot, he stood. And he stared. I don't know if Mark felt that feeling we all get when we know someone is staring, but soon he looked down and made eye contact with an admiring young fan. Mark smiled at the boy, and then went on talking to the crowd. Colby's next report back to me was to report this "thrill of his lifetime," as he called it.

When at last we made it to the front of the line to meet Rusty Wallace, Colby wanted a picture. This would be tricky, since the line must keep moving, and nobody else was taking pictures. We hatched a plan that would need to be executed perfectly, as we'd have but one chance.

With precision choreography, Colby jumped up on the platform where Rusty sat. There was no more than half an inch on which to balance himself, so he grabbed the table for dear life. Rusty, upon hearing his name shrieked by a giddy mom (that would be me), looked up and obliged us with a smile. We moved along with our autographs, high-fiving one another at what we'd accomplished.

Race day might have paled in comparison to seeing the drivers we root for week after week, up close and personal. Still, my son pressed his little body against the fence to get as close as he could to Jeff Gordon after his introduction, and snapped picture after picture of his favorite driver as he drove by waving to the crowd.

Jeff went on to win that day, and although I was tired with aching feet, suffering the effects of sleep deprivation and a weekend of junk food, I smile whenever I hear Colby tell people about his race experience. He always says the same thing: "I met Rusty Wallace, Mark Martin smiled at me, and Jeff Gordon *WON!*"

There you have it, the perfect weekend for any ten-year-old race fan. I was just lucky enough to share the joy.

Carol Einarsson

He Felt It

I went turkey hunting with Dale one time. It was phenomenal. It's probably the best experience I ever had in sixteen or seventeen years because I had the rare opportunity to see him just as a man. He didn't even talk about racing. We were in Montgomery, Alabama, for two days. It was funny. I had just started dating my wife. He was giving me marriage advice—relationship advice. He said, "Hey Byrnes, do you love that girl, Karen?"

I said, "Well, yeah, I think I do, Dale."

He said, "Marry her, do it now." I mean he was just very down-to-earth about that.

We went out about midnight in his Blazer. There were about three hundred acres of nothing but wilderness. He turned the headlights off, and it was pitch dark. We went flying around that farm. We could see absolutely nothing, and he was driving across dry river beds and up hills; we were even airborne a couple of times. I was scared to death for a minute, and then I thought, *You know what, this guy's the greatest driver in the world.* After that experience with Dale, I always believed that when he had a steering wheel in his hands, he could just feel and see things that you and I never will. He could just feel it.

Steve Byrnes

One Moment with Kyle Petty

The weekend of the Coca-Cola 600 in Charlotte was an eventful one for me. It was my first time in Charlotte, my first trip to North Carolina and my first visit to any race shop. I also experienced track grit flying into my face for the first time. Being on row 5 was thrilling, to say the least. It was also the weekend of the only experience that has ever caused me to break down into tears in front of two hundred people. No, I wasn't throwing a temper tantrum. No, I didn't miss meeting Hank Parker Jr. I cried because Kyle Petty changed my life in the span of one moment.

I stood in line for quite some time to meet Kyle. I had met him twice before, and I'd always been impressed by his attitude and courtesy to fans. In my hands I held the book *From the Heart of Racing,* which included a story I wrote entitled "Someone I Never Knew" a few weeks after the death of Adam Petty. In it, I describe how Adam had changed my life by the way he lived his life. Little did I know that, in a few moments, Kyle would change mine in the very same way.

When I reached Kyle, I showed him my story and told him I had written it about Adam. He kept saying, "That is so cool." He signed the page, then I went behind the table to where Kyle was sitting so my dad could take our picture. I bent down to be on Kyle's level. The second after Dad had snapped the picture, Kyle softly whispered, "God bless you." Then he hugged me. Without a word, without a sign, Kyle Petty wrapped his arms around me, and in that moment I knew that everything was going to be okay.

I made it safely out of Kyle's line of sight before the tears overflowed. I did not want him to see me crying. I never cry in front of people! I even hate for my mother to see me crying. Surprisingly, I had not cried since before the anniversary of Adam's death on May 12. All at once, bottled emotions got the best of me, and I let the tears fall. It didn't matter who was watching. No, not much mattered at that moment.

In the end, Kyle didn't make the race at Charlotte, and I didn't get to see him steer that #45 around the track. But I did get to see a Kyle Petty I have never seen before. That Kyle Petty changed my life with one action, in a single moment. Sometimes, something happens that leaves writers without words. For me, that moment came the first time I visited Charlotte, the third time I saw Kyle Petty. I am not ashamed that I cried in front of those two hundred people. I am only thankful that I was blessed with an amazing memory to carry with me as long as I live—all because of Kyle and Adam and a moment beyond words.

Jenni Thompson

Hot Wheels

Is it normal for a spectator sport to totally captivate you? So quickly? Is there something wrong with me? I turn down baby showers and early dinners out. Is that normal? How did this happen? I mean, it's just cars going in circles, right?

Honestly, I've got this bad. I didn't know how badly until Saturday night. About forty-five minutes into the race there was a knock on the door. It was too late to switch off the lights and hit the mute button. So I opened the door to a trio of Jehovah's Witnesses. I tried to put them off. I told them about the two large dogs I owned and the skyrocketing price of dog food (they didn't get it). I offered them twenty-five dollars, no questions asked. I even told them about the serial killer who walks the block every Saturday night. They just don't scare easy. I admire that kind of faith. You just can't run 'em off!

So I sat down with them trying to be polite. That's when things went south. I was giving myself a headache with one eye on the TV and one on the "leader of the Jehovah's Witnesses." I tried, really I did, but, well . . . when the next crash happened, I shushed them and turned the volume back up to a level that made the dogs howl. I *had* to see who was in the crash and what caused it! After I assured myself that Kevin "Hot Wheels" Harvick wasn't involved by watching it over three times (I don't trust those new announcers yet) I repeatedly hugged the leader and told him to thank whatever deity or supreme being he worked for. He seemed quite interested in whatever it was that brought out that much emotion in me. I sat them all down and said, "Just watch."

Well, let me tell you right now, I have someone to watch the race with next Sunday! And these guys have got connections to "The Big Guy." So when "Hot Wheels" takes his *next* checkered flag . . . and he lets the smoke roll . . . it will give a whole new meaning to the phrase "Holy Smoke."

Laura Kelly

Reprinted by permission of Mike Smith, Las Vegas Sun.

For Dale

This is for the one who could see air,
The one who passed cars like they weren't there.
This is for the one we all wished we could be,
This one goes out to the black number three.
You were the one we thought could never die,
And now you're with Neil, racin' in the sky.
Dale, you were hated, loved and everything in-between,
But no one can deny you're the best we've ever seen.
We grieve for your children, your wife and your fans,
Even tears gather for those filling the stands.
Racing continues, something we all must do,
Yet every race will be missing someone—you.
So here's to The Intimidator we fondly call Dale,
Who rattled cages and entertained us so well.
Here's to seventy-six wins and trophies galore,
Here's to exiting by window and not by the door.
Here's to the man so many held dear,
Who would've won number eight this year?
But God waved the calling, checkered you to heaven,
Where he gave you the eighth, replacing all seven.

Jenni Thompson

The Anonymous Donor

It has been my pleasure to help facilitate and coordinate donations and sponsorships on behalf of Speedway Children's Charities over the last six years as national marketing director. All of the funds are deeply appreciated and always come from the heart from both donors and sponsors alike, no matter the amount of the contribution.

One donation that sticks in my mind, however, is a donation that comes in to us every six to eight weeks. It has no return address, usually has a small drawing on the envelope (obviously a children's drawing) and a cashier's check for ten dollars mailed from Harrisburg, North Carolina. It definitely is not the largest donation we receive throughout the month, but it's one that touches all the employees here at the Speedway Children's Charities every time it's received.

The reason it means so much to us is twofold. One, somewhere out there is an adult(s) who has taken the time to drive the child to the convenience store that the cashier's check is drawn on, making the act of giving a special activity. Second, the child never leaves a name or return address; he or she just gives unconditionally to other children in need. Speedway Children's Charities is fortunate to have such supporters as this child and his or her parents; I only hope that I can raise my own children to know what the true meaning of giving is, as our anonymous donor does.

Deb Wilson

The Ron Kumitch Story

This is not a story with a happy ending; it's a story about one.

Ron Kumitch was a forty-one-year-old Jeff Gordon fan living in Edmonton, Alberta, Canada, who had never been to a NASCAR race in person.

During the summer of 2001, Kumitch's son Rob was determined to change that. But time was of the essence.

Ron Kumitch had cancer of the lymphoid system, and the treatments had not produced the kind of results the family was looking for. The prognosis was grim.

Rob Kumitch sat down at his computer to write an e-mail that he hoped he could somehow get Gordon to see, hoping the driver who was on his way to his fourth career NASCAR Winston Cup championship could help.

"I don't even know if Jeff Gordon will be the one reading this," he wrote, "but if he is not, I hope that whoever is could find it in his heart to make sure he does."

Rob sent his e-mail to a reporter whose NASCAR coverage he and his father had read on the Internet.

"We have planned a last vacation—hopefully not—for November," he wrote. "We would like to attend a NASCAR race weekend."

He was hoping Gordon, or somebody who read the e-mail, could arrange for race tickets for him and his brother, Adam, to bring their parents Ron and Bev to one of the season's final two races at Homestead Miami Speedway or Atlanta Motor Speedway.

"We can pay you back when we get there," Rob Kumitch wrote in the message addressed directly to Gordon. "And if at all possible, is there a chance you may be able to meet my father on race weekend?

"The reason I ask you to do this for me is because as a driver I'm sure you can do more for us than anyone else. I pray that you can help us. If you can't, then I wish you all the luck for the remainder of the season and in your hunt for the championship."

The reporter who got the e-mail forwarded it along to the public-relations staff that handles dozens of similar requests for Gordon each week. Gordon is involved with the Make-A-Wish Foundation, a group that grants the wishes of critically ill children, and meets with several of those children virtually every weekend during the NASCAR season.

The message also was forwarded to a writer from the *Atlanta Journal-Constitution* and to the staff at the Atlanta racetrack.

A few weeks before the season's final race, Rob Kumitch heard from Kathy Boyd of the Jeff Gordon Foundation, who had arranged for Ron Kumitch and the rest of the family to meet the driver on Saturday, the day before the season finale. He sent one more e-mail to make sure he'd be able to get the tickets to get his family inside the track for that meeting. After making contact with Angela Clare, the Atlanta track's public-relations manager, all of the details were worked out.

On November 16, 2001, the Kumitch family flew from Canada to Atlanta, arriving just before midnight. The next morning, they drove to the track about twenty-five miles south of the city in Hampton, Georgia, and picked up their tickets and garage passes. After watching some of the race practice, they went to the drivers' motor-home lot to wait with three other families who had similar reasons for being there.

"All of a sudden we heard 'Jeff! Jeff!' being yelled by many fans, and then Jeff came around the corner," Rob Kumitch said. "I saw my father's face light up like never before. Even though Jeff had three other groups to meet with, he still took a good twenty minutes to meet with my father and then twenty minutes each for the other groups. He talked with my father and signed everything that we handed him."

It had been a memorable day. The Kumitch family went back to their hotel near the Atlanta airport, eagerly anticipating Sunday's race in which they would get to see Gordon cap off another championship season.

On Sunday morning, however, Ron Kumitch was very weak. Rob called the airline and arranged for the family to leave for home later that day, but Ron insisted that Rob and Adam stay for the race. "He felt that he could live the race through our eyes," Rob said.

That afternoon, about the time Ron and Bev Kumitch began their flight home, Gordon finished sixth in the NAPA 500 and wrapped up the 2001 NASCAR Winston Cup championship. Rob and Adam went home on Monday, looking forward to telling their father all about it.

Rob and Adam got home at 3:30 P.M.

Two hours later, Ron Kumitch died.

"My father passed away in our house and in our arms, right after hearing our stories of how much fun the race was and how well Jeff did," Rob Kumitch said. "With how busy Jeff's schedule is and how much he still needed to do that morning, the fact that he took so much time out of his day to spend with his fans is unbelievable.

"My father got to be one of the few who could say he lived his dream and met his hero. He passed away a happy man."

David Poole

The Rules of the Game

It's time to get out the lawyers. Some people have pre-nuptial agreements: I'm taking it a step further. I need one pre-dating exclusively agreement, as I have yet again found someone who knows nothing about racing. If anyone else finds themselves in the same predicament, feel free to use this.

Pre-Dating Exclusively Agreement

1. *Before I agree to date you and only you, you must read and agree to all statements in this contract. By signing below, you acknowledge all statements and take full responsibility to ensure they are maintained. By not signing this agreement, dating exclusively is null and void. This contract is nonnegotiable.*

2. *If you stop insulting stock-car racing and concede it is a real sport, that it takes talent and skill, I will stop calling your WWE wrestling a badly choreographed soap opera with untalented actors. However, I won't stop thinking it.*

3. *If you take a genuine interest in racing, I will be more than happy to help you gain an intimate understanding of the sport.*

4. *Events and activities are to be planned around NASCAR races. So learn the race schedule. Under special circumstances, this may not apply. However, the race I am going to miss must be taped using two VCRs (just in case one fails).* **NO** *special circumstances will be considered for the following races: Daytona 500 and the Bristol night race! If I am not watching them via satellite live, then I will be at the track watching them.*

5. *You already know about the normal holidays: Easter, Labor Day, Thanksgiving, Christmas and New Year's. I have two other holidays: Speed Weeks and Daytona. Strict adherence to the observation of these holidays must be maintained!*

6. *During a race I do not accept phone calls. No matter how many times you call, I will not answer.*

7. *If you are in my presence while watching a race, please observe the following: Do not touch the remote, television, receiver or VCR. Doing so will result in serious injury or worse. Do not talk during the race. I will get duct tape out if necessary. Commercial breaks are the only times you may attempt to have a conversation with me. You must sit a minimum of five feet away from me. This is partially for your own safety. If during a race, you are in a romantic mood, don't bother attempting to share it with me. Take a cold shower till the race is over.*

8. *While it seems inevitable that couples share things, there are some things I won't share. My racing apparel is off limits;* do not touch it *(even if you are frozen and they are the only things left in the closet).*

9. *See #8 and substitute racing collection for racing apparel.*

10. *See #8 and substitute racing books and magazines for racing apparel.*

11. *While you may find Jamaica a romantic vacation spot, I find Martinsville, Bristol, Loudon, Richmond and locales housing race shops or tracks romantic vacation spots.*

12. *When I take my vacation time, I will be visiting one or more of the locales mentioned in #11. You don't expect me to go deer hunting, and I don't expect you to spend the day at DEI or Rockingham.*

13. *If we break up and there is property to be divided, you may request the return of anything you gave me, excluding racing-related items. You may keep anything I gave you, except for the racing items. All items must be in original condition.*

14. *In the event of cohabitation, I require one room solely for the purposes of holding and displaying my race-related stuff. The smallest room will not be acceptable.*

15. *If it comes down to a choice between you and racing— racing will win.*

16. *If the opportunity arises that I can get tickets to the Bristol race under the lights, complete with garage access, I will do anything for them. If it requires your assistance, you will do anything to ensure I get them.*

17. *If it comes down to a choice between you and Dale Jr.—Dale Jr. wins.*

By signing below, you have read and agreed to all terms set forth in this contract. Please note that there may be further additions to this contract at any time.

I should be single by the weekend.

Heather McGee

"He's so romantic! On our first date,
he spelled out my name in skid marks."

Reprinted by permission of Jonny Hawkins.

4

FROM
THE HEART

To me, the real heroes are the people who do worthwhile things without the thought of monetary gain.

Benny Parsons

A Change in Outlook

It was a day in late May when my outlook on life was changed by a single Outlook e-mail message. It was my first day back at work from maternity leave after having my first child, a beautiful baby girl named Kaitlyn Rose. I worked for Ford Credit Racing as a motorsport specialist at Ford World Headquarters located just outside of Detroit. My job was to help Ford Credit get the most out of its sponsorship of NASCAR driver Dale Jarrett and his #88 Ford Taurus team. One of the programs I worked on, my brainchild and pet program, was Race Fans for a Cure®, an initiative dedicated to raising awareness of breast cancer among race fans while raising money to help find a cure.

One of the newest aspects of this program was the launch of a Web site, *www.racefansforacure.com*, through which race fans around the country could learn about the program, get information, share their stories and even donate to the cause. Although the site was just getting started when I returned from leave, we were already starting to receive e-mail messages from fans, breast-cancer survivors and supporters of the cause. When I opened the mailbox on that first day back, the following message was waiting:

Name: Jenny Meyer
City: Hope
State: Idaho
Subject: Thank you and see you soon!

Comments: *In April of 2000, I was diagnosed with inflammatory breast cancer. I was only twenty-six at the time and pregnant with our first child. Needless to say, it was a very scary time for my husband and me. With no cancer in my family and being active and athletic, it was a complete shock.*

I began chemotherapy right away and continued until the third trimester of our pregnancy. I had a mastectomy in August and would resume chemo once our baby was born. On November 11, we had a baby girl, Grace Katherine. She was an absolute miracle that God provided. A few weeks later, I started chemo again, in addition to radiation. Now, over a year later, we're finished with treatment and apparently cancer-free! In celebration of that, my husband and I booked a trip to Phoenix in October! I am so excited to see it all in person. I got addicted to NASCAR while I battled the cancer. I look forward to every race and can't begin to tell you how thrilled we are that I'll be able to see it all happen live.

It's only appropriate that I do it in October (National Breast Cancer Awareness Month) and I see it's one of the Race Fans for a Cure events. I know it's a long shot, but if there were any way I could personally thank Kelley Jarrett for all she does, I would love the opportunity. It's just that Ford and the Jarretts do so much, they need to know how much it means to a person who has her whole life ahead of her due to the advances in research. To be able to fight and win is such an incredible feeling. I just want to thank you for all the hard

*work that you do. It means so much to a survivor. See
you in Phoenix.*

*With sincere gratitude,
Jenny Meyer*

Needless to say, it was difficult to keep the tears from
flowing after I read Jenny's message. It was also eerily
coincidental that we were both twenty-six, new moms
and both named Jenny. I think that's part of the reason
Jenny's story hit me so hard.

Even though I had come up with the concept for the
Race Fans for a Cure® program and was involved in the
breast-cancer cause, I never considered that breast cancer
could happen to me, especially being only twenty-six. Yet
here was a woman, so incredibly like myself, who had to
fight that battle on top of all the challenges that come
with pregnancy and motherhood.

It took me a few days to respond to Jenny's note, not
because I couldn't help her. I knew setting up a meeting
in Phoenix with Kelley Jarrett wouldn't be a problem. If
she were going to be at the race, she'd willingly come to
the booth as she had at various other Race Fans for a Cure®
events in the past. The issue was that I didn't know quite
how to respond to Jenny. When I did write her back, I fell
back on what I knew: I based my e-mail on the fact that I
would see what I could do to set up the meeting with
Kelley and that I would get back to her. What I didn't
expect was that in the weeks between that initial e-mail in
May and the race in October, Jenny and I would become
such good friends, sharing baby pictures, motherhood
stories, basically sharing our lives over e-mail.

As the weeks between May and October narrowed, we
started working out the final details of the trip to Phoenix.
Kelley Jarrett had said that she would love to meet Jenny

and that she would be happy to stop by the Race Fans for a Cure® booth on Saturday. I also secured garage credentials for Jenny and her husband, Jeff, so they could get the insider's view of things. When Saturday finally came, I remember being swamped by eager donors, passing out ribbons for them to personalize and collecting donations when I heard a voice say "Jen Riley?" I looked up, and standing in front of me was a beautiful, vibrant young woman with short brown hair and a questioning look on her face, as if to say, "Am I in the right place?" "Jenny Meyer!" I shouted and rushed forward to give her a hug. It was as if we'd known each other forever, while just meeting in person for the first time.

The day was rushed, and we had huge lines at the booth when Kelley Jarrett got there. I made sure Jenny was right up front to meet Kelley, get her autograph and tell her what she had wanted to say. We got to talk for a few minutes in the back of the booth, but then it was back to business, me collecting donations and Jenny saving her husband from standing by himself outside the tent where he waited not wanting to interrupt us. It was short but sweet, and really brought home the meaning of what we were doing with Race Fans for a Cure® and why it was so important.

In an e-mail I received from Jenny after returning from Phoenix, she described in her own words why programs like Race Fans for a Cure® are so important.

I became a huge fan of Dale Jarrett because of all the work he does for the Susan G. Komen Breast Cancer Foundation. Due to research, I wasn't told to terminate my baby; we would wait to see how everything went. So due to the funds provided by Ford and the Jarretts, research can continue. That's very important to me because my fight is long from over. I want to be able to take Grace to her first day of kindergarten. According to the odds that I was given, there is a 70 percent chance of that not happening. Research and advances in this field decrease those odds, and I need to depend on that. Most importantly, I made a connection with someone halfway across the country and walked away with a wonderful new friend. That's the best part.

Jenny and I have corresponded regularly via e-mail since then and have continued our long-distance relationship. And I can't help thinking about her and little Grace every time I look at my own daughter, thinking of all the blessings in my life and how important it is to share them with the world. I have no doubt that Jenny will take Grace to her first day of kindergarten, that she will see her off to her senior prom and cry tears of joy as she watches her walk down the aisle on her wedding day. Jenny is a survivor, and I know that stories like hers will open hearts and pocketbooks so that some day there will be a cure for breast cancer, and so that daughters like Grace and Kaitlyn will have nothing to fear from it.

Jennifer Riley and Jennifer Meyer

Hard Racer, Soft Heart

Every day, try to help someone who can't recip-rocate your kindness.

Coach John Wooden

If the word "firebrand" were used in relation to one NASCAR driver, the image of Tony Stewart would come to mind for many fans. Stewart's glorious achievements on the tracks of the land are equaled only by his struggles to keep his substantial temper in check once the races are over.

There is another side to Tony Stewart, one he is reluctant to put on public display. If the truth be known, Stewart is just an old softie. He is as sentimental as a kindly grandfather and as sensitive as a swollen thumb. No one regrets his transgressions more than Stewart, who wakes up the morning after a fiery episode as penitent as a drunkard feeling the aftereffects of a bender.

It is fairly common knowledge that Stewart donated $240,000 toward the construction of the Victory Junction Gang Camp, founded by Kyle Petty in memory of his late son, Adam. What is not widely known is the inspiration for that contribution, which came from Stewart's winnings in the 2001 Indianapolis 500 and the corporate largesse of his NASCAR Winston Cup sponsor, Home Depot.

Stewart was testing his #20 Pontiac at an obscure track in Lakeland, Florida, when he heard a story on the radio about an abandoned dog that had been chained up and left to starve by its owners. A local humane society had found the poor mutt near death and was trying to restore it to health.

Stewart, a dog lover, impetuously dialed the phone number that had been repeated on the broadcast and expressed his desire to pay whatever cost was needed to restore the ailing dog to health. Informed that local citizens had already contributed more than what was needed, Stewart asked how much had been raised and insisted on giving an equal amount for the establishment of a fund to aid other unfortunate canines.

An associate of Stewart mentioned the episode in passing to an official of Home Depot, who, in turn, contacted Stewart to inform him that the company had a fund for charitable donations and would be glad to assist him in any contributions he found compelling.

That offer got Stewart to thinking, and Petty's Victory Junction Gang was what he came up with.

As with everything else, when Stewart made his donation, he did it on a grand scale. Few others know the story because Stewart seems somewhat reluctant to talk about it. He did what he did out of personal compassion, not because he wanted to receive credit or have his name in the paper.

Of course, the story got out, but many other touching stories about Stewart have not.

Monte Dutton

Gentleman Ned

Most new race fans know Ned Jarrett as the baritone-voiced announcer who worked so many years for CBS and ESPN before retiring at the end of the 2000 season. Most also realize that Ned is 1999 NASCAR Winston Cup champion Dale Jarrett's father. But what some newer fans may not know is that in his time Ned Jarrett was a very fine racer himself who won a total of four NASCAR championships: two in the Sportsman (now Busch) Division and two in the top tier Grand National (now NASCAR Winston Cup) Division. Throughout his entire career, in addition to being a great driver and broadcaster, he was also a fine gentleman.

Surprisingly, though, despite his reputation as a straight shooter, Jarrett's career in the Grand National Division started with a bad check. Jarrett had won the Sportsman championship in 1957 and 1958 and was eager to race in the Grand National Division. No car owners approached him offering a ride so one Friday afternoon after the banks had closed, Jarrett wrote a check to a gentleman for a race-ready Ford. Unfortunately, there wasn't enough money in Jarrett's account to cover the check, but his plan was simple. If he won the two Grand

National races that weekend at Myrtle Beach, South Carolina, and Charlotte, North Carolina, both of them dirt tracks, he would have enough money to make the check good before the bank opened Monday morning.

Jarrett did, in fact, win the Myrtle Beach race, but he paid a terrible price for it. In that era there were no custom racing steering wheels, and the skinny, plastic, Detroit-issued steering wheels grew slippery under a driver's sweaty palms. It was common practice to wrap the steering wheel in electrical tape to give the driver more grip. Properly done, the wheel was wrapped in a counterclockwise direction, but one of Jarrett's well-meaning helpers wrapped the steering wheel the wrong way. Thus each time Ned let the wheel slip through his fingers exiting a corner, the raised edges of the tape chewed savagely away at his fingers and palms. After the 200-lap race, Jarrett's flesh was chewed down to the bone in places and the footwell of the car was awash in blood. Yet somehow he won that race anyway.

In order to cover the check, Jarrett not only had to race but win the next day, even with his hands in such terrible shape. And win he did, with a little help from his friends. Joe Weatherly wasn't entered to race that day, but he took over for Jarrett as a relief driver midway through the race. When Junior Johnson, the former driver of the #11 Ford, blew an engine later in the race, he took the wheel of Jarrett's car during a caution period and drove it to the victory, thus giving Jarrett the money needed to cover the check.

Despite its unorthodox start, Jarrett went on to have a successful Grand National career. In 1961 he won the Grand National title piloting a Chevy. He wanted to represent the sport well as its champion, but was shy by nature and not well-spoken. So Ned did something unheard-of for a race-car driver in that era—he took a Dale

NASCAR Photography/Sherryl Creekmore

NASCAR Photography/Sherryl Creekmore

NIGHT RACING

SAFETY FIRST

NASCAR Photography/Sherryl Creekmore

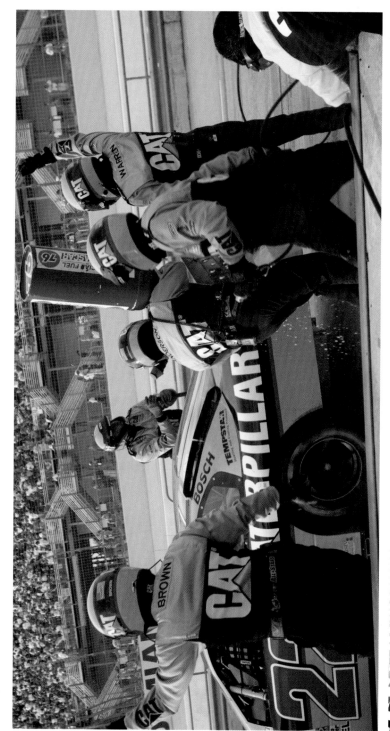

TEAMWORK WORKS

NASCAR Photography/Sherryl Creekmore

FOUNDERS OF VICTORY JUNCTION GANG CAMP

NASCAR Photography/Sherryl Creekmore

ALMOST 200 MPH AND ONLY INCHES FROM THE COMPETITION

NASCAR Photography/Sherryl Creekmore

MID-RACE TIRE CHANGE

NASCAR Photography/Sherryl Creekmore

NASCAR Photography/Sherryl Creekmore

RUNNING THREE WIDE

TEAMMATES — MICHAEL WALTRIP & DALE EARNHARDT JR.

THE DAYTONA 500 — "PINNACLE OF THE SPORT"

NASCAR Photography/Sherryl Creekmore

TERESA EARNHARDT & DALE EARNHARDT JR.

▰▰▰ **PIT-ROW FRENZY**

BOBBY LABONTE, EYES OF A CHAMPION

TONY STEWART, 2002 NASCAR WINSTON CUP CHAMPION

MICHAEL WALTRIP — 2003 DAYTONA 500
VICTORY CELEBRATION

JEREMY MAYFIELD SHOWING HIS PRIDE

Carnegie public-speaking course, which would one day lead to his broadcast career. (Not everyone was convinced Jarrett's deep drawl would be understood by all audiences. In the movie "Last American Hero," Ned appears as himself as a race announcer, but another voice was dubbed over his own out of fear Northerners wouldn't be able to understand him.)

Jarrett used his training and gift at public speaking to promote many causes, but especially his deeply held faith in God. On the morning of September 6, 1965, Jarrett spoke to a group of Boy Scouts on the power of prayer. His victory that day in the Southern 500 was a convincing upholding of his conviction.

Although he rarely discussed it, Ned Jarrett once risked his own life at a racetrack to try to save the life of a friend. Jarrett and Junior Johnson were racing hard for position early in the 1964 World 600. The two cars tangled and spun out of control. Fireball Roberts, driving what was to have been his last season prior to retirement, tried to avoid the wreck and spun into an opening in the wall that allowed spectators to cross over the track into the infield before and after the race. Roberts' car rolled over and exploded into flames.

Jarrett's car was also engulfed in fire, but it remained right side up. Jarrett leapt from his car, rushed over and pulled Roberts to safety. The two of them tore away at burning sections of Roberts' driving uniform. Ultimately, Roberts died of complications from the burns he suffered, but had Jarrett not gone to his aid, Roberts would most likely have burned to death in front of the crowd that Memorial Day weekend.

Jarrett retired from driving after the 1966 season. Eventually, he got into race broadcasting and started a second highly successful career. Working the ESPN booth, Jarrett called the first race won by his son Dale (Michigan,

1991) and Dale's first Daytona 500 triumph in 1993. On CBS, while most race fans enjoyed listening to an emotional Ned calling the final laps of the Daytona 500 as his son held off a determined charge from Dale Earnhardt, Ned felt he'd lapsed professionally by rooting so openly for his son. The following weekend he sought out Dale Earnhardt to apologize for the gaffe, but The Intimidator just smiled. "Ned, don't forget, I'm a daddy, too."

But Jarrett repeated the apology because he was a great driver, broadcaster, daddy—and gentleman.

Matt McLaughlin

Ground Zero

A brave heart is a powerful weapon.

H. Jackson Brown Jr.

I didn't feel that I deserved to be there. This was a sacred place where family members and friends who had lost loved ones needed to be, and yet I am glad that I got to go and see it. Glad that I was able to experience first-hand this unforgettable place.

Rick Hendrick and I arrived only a few weeks after the terrorist attacks on the World Trade Center. The destruction was so massive that it's difficult to describe. I had heard many claims that television and pictures cannot grasp the full impact of Ground Zero, and now I knew what they meant.

Before me was a massive pile of grotesquely twisted metal and debris. The surrounding buildings were just burnt-out shells. The buildings that were spared the fire had massive gashes. The primary debris field (the footings of the Twin Towers) still burned, and the air was full of an unpleasant smell. Cranes and trucks of every size removed large pieces from what were once two beautiful skyscrapers. All that was left was rubble.

I was full of many different emotions, but mostly sadness and anger. I had the honor of meeting and speaking with many of the emergency and rescue personnel, construction crews and volunteers. They were incredibly devoted and brave people. It made me feel strange when, as we departed, they thanked *us* for visiting. I tried sheepishly to explain that it was us who needed to express our gratitude to them.

As we were leaving, we saw so many people trying to get a look at the wreckage and to pay their respects and get a realization of what took place here. I wondered if everyone who could see what we just saw would even want to look anymore.

Three thousand heroes died here—three thousand who made the ultimate sacrifice and paid the ultimate price. They helped us learn what true courage and strength we have as a people. The word "hero" was redefined in this senseless tragedy. I pray we never forget.

Jeff Gordon

Young 'Sponsor' Helps Allison's Team

Love cures people—both the ones who give it and the ones who receive it.

Dr. Karl Menninger

Chris Gregory, barely able to contain his enthusiasm, hurried his parents and track escorts across the garage area to where the Bobby Allison Motorsports transporter sat between turns three and four.

It was a cloudy and unseasonably chilly day but Chris' smile and abundant energy brought a special warmth to those standing nearby who could hear what the nine-year-old had to say to the 1983 NASCAR Winston Cup champion.

Clutching a precious white envelope in his hands, the boy looked up at Bobby and said, "This is $25 and some change, and I would like to donate this to you."

"Well, thank you," Allison replied in a kind, fatherly voice. "Let me tell you, I really appreciate that."

Chris then started to talk about how special Bobby's son Davey had been to him, a memory that brought tears to the child's eyes. Davey Allison, who suffered fatal injuries in a helicopter crash last year, had been Chris' favorite driver.

"Davey was a neat guy, wasn't he?" Bobby said.

"He sure was," Chris said as he wiped tears away with his left arm.

"You never got to meet Clifford, did you?" Bobby asked, referring to Davey's younger brother who was killed in 1992.

Chris shook his head no.

It was a comforting encounter for Allison, whose own driving career ended in a 1988 crash that seriously injured him, and who lost his close friend and former protege, Neil Bonnett, earlier this year.

"Clifford was a neat guy, too," Bobby said as he put his arm around the boy.

"Yeah, I bet he was," Chris said, taking a deep breath.

"And we miss Davey, and we miss Clifford, and we miss Neil. And I really appreciate the help," Bobby told Chris.

"I really hope you get a sponsor," Chris said, wiping more tears from his eyes.

"Thank you," Bobby replied as he gave the boy a strong hug.

"You're welcome," Chris answered.

There's more to this story, however, than a short but cherished conversation between a young boy and his hero's father.

Chris' parents didn't give him the money for him to hand to Bobby. The child earned it shoveling snow, a lot of snow, in his hometown of Waynesboro, Va.

Initially, Chris was earning the money for himself. His parents, Lynne and Matt Gregory, told him a weekend trip had been planned for the April Martinsville race, so Chris decided to make extra money so he could buy souvenirs. But then one day, while looking at the numerous racing photographs decorating his bedroom wall, he changed his mind and decided instead of spending the money on himself, whatever he earned would go to Allison, who has no full-time sponsor for his NASCAR Winston Cup team.

"I was looking at those pictures thinking of Davey and I just thought I oughta give this money to Bobby because I think it would really help," the Gregorys' only child said, noting he'd earned about $10 or $15 when he made his decision.

"I really miss Davey a lot. I met Davey one time and that was when he was in Richmond. My mom picked me up at school and didn't tell me where we were going. I kept asking and she said it was a surprise, to just wait and I'd find out. When we got there I saw Davey's show car and I said, 'Mom, Davey's here, right?' And she said, 'Yeah.' That was the only time I ever met Davey and I really miss him."

Now Chris' favorite drivers are Ernie Irvan, Rusty Wallace, Jeff Gordon, Mark Martin—"all the good guys," is the way he explains it

Chris, who became interested in racing about three years ago, didn't have a special fee for his snow shoveling service. "I just took whatever I got," he said. And shoveling the snow was in addition to his regular chores around the house, which include making his bed, helping his mother with the laundry and assisting his dad with mowing the grass.

Anyone who doubted the moment with Chris was special to Bobby needed only to look into Allison's eyes to see how deeply the boy's actions touched him.

Chris asked if he could put his signature on Bobby's No. 12 Ford— "really, really small" where no one would notice, "but it would be there." Without hesitation, Allison provided the youngster with a special pen to use for inscribing his name in gold ink and escorted him to the frontstretch pit where the black car was parked.

"It's a really special feeling that our efforts and involvement in this sport have reached out to even touch a youngster to the point that they would go earn money, bring it and say to put that toward paying the bills on the car," Allison said.

"I've never had anything like that happen before. I've had some youngsters offer help and offer to do work on the car or do work at the shop in terms of just trying to help. But for a youngster to have gone and earned some money by doing a chore and then say put that to the car. . . .

"It's a deal that allows you to appreciate people and allows you to appreciate the way people feel about this sport."

Deb Williams

Pray for Kyle

Courage is grace under pressure.

Ernest Hemingway

I remember sitting in the middle of my hometown base-ball diamond one hot summer day when I was a kid, head between my knees, glove over my head and tears of frus-tration at my inability to hit a curveball streaming down my dirty cheeks.

Nothing anyone could have said right then could possibly have suppressed my anger. I didn't care if Dale Murphy himself had appeared to tell me that he couldn't hit a curveball when he was a kid. I was furious, and there was no changing it.

Then I smelled my dad's cologne.

He crouched down beside me, snow cone in one hand, glove in the other, and sat on second base. He assured me my lack of prowess at hitting the "old number 2" hadn't marked the demise of my young career, and that we'd work on it until I ripped every last one of them.

We spent hours working on it, so much that my old man is probably incapable of throwing a baseball anymore. But you know what? I learned how to knock the crap out of a curveball that day, and seeing him beam with pride every time I did so made it obvious to me that a mutilated rotator cuff was totally worth it to him.

That's a lot like Kyle Petty. Most of his NASCAR Winston Cup dreams having already been fulfilled, sacrificing any remaining glory to help his son achieve his high-speed hopes and dreams.

Kyle tossed his own career aside to assure that Adam's would prosper. He was perfectly content with that. It was obvious in the way he carried himself, how he tripped over himself with glee at how well his son was performing in a race car.

Then the unthinkable happened.

As the NASCAR Winston Cup Series steered to Loudon, New Hampshire, for Sunday's New England 300, Petty faced the stiffest test of his lengthy career. For the first time, he returned to the racetrack that claimed his eldest son's life and, sadly enough, a significant part of his own.

Kyle is a wonderful man, arguably the most giving, caring, thoughtful man ever to grace the racetrack. When his son was so tragically taken from him, a part of him died as well. Still, he gives far more to others than he gives to himself.

He doesn't want to give to himself. He doesn't want to feel whole. He'll never get over Adam's death, doesn't want to. He feels that the day he wakes up and doesn't hurt, that Adam isn't as close to him as he once was.

That is so, so sad.

July 7 was one of the greatest father/son days in NASCAR history. Ricky Hendrick won the inaugural NASCAR Craftsman Truck Series race at Kansas City with his father on hand to celebrate.

Jon Wood finished fourth in that same race, his father Eddie calling countless times from Daytona to check in on his son's progress. In one of the most poignant moments in NASCAR history, Dale Earnhardt Jr. won the Pepsi 400 that night. You know his daddy was smiling.

After the 400, I remember being so happy for all three of those kids. I remember thinking how awesome it must have been for those fathers to experience such a triumphant day with their sons. I called my father to discuss it with him, and during our conversation I remember thinking about Kyle.

He wanted moments like that with Adam so badly.

Sometimes life has its own curveballs.

Marty Smith

Reprinted by permission of Mike Smith, Las Vegas Sun.

His Father's Son

I could feel the emotion in the air, as thick and heavy as a Florida summer night. I was part of the tens of thousands of NASCAR fans who were returning to Daytona for the Pepsi 400, only five months since the tragic death of the sports' hero, Dale Earnhardt, at the same track.

The stage was set for what would be an opportunity for all of us, in fact the entire NASCAR world, to mourn the loss of the man who epitomized the sports' image. This would be the chance for a mass catharsis that all too clearly underscores the high-speed drama of auto racing. Perhaps this is why the sport is so beloved by race fans, because NASCAR by its very nature is a metaphor for life.

Prior to the race, large crowds had gathered outside of turn 4 where Earnhardt's car had crashed into the wall on the final lap of the Daytona 500. The Intimidator was in third place at the time, holding off all pursuers while protecting the first-place finish of teammates Michael Waltrip and the second-place finish of his son, Dale Earnhardt Jr.

Against this somber backdrop an unbelievable sporting event was unfolding at the Pepsi 400. Dale Earnhardt Jr. clearly had the best car all night. He led an incredible 116 of 160 laps, but the most dramatic twist came in the final minutes of the race. As anyone who has ever been to a NASCAR race knows, the final minutes of a NASCAR race are never spent sitting down, and Dale Earnhardt Jr. would give us all good reason to spring to our feet in excitement. Earnhardt Jr. had been pushed back to seventh place for the restart after a late yellow flag. There were only nine laps left in the race, and many people all but conceded Junior's fate as a gallant effort. Then with only four and a half laps left, Dale Earnhardt Jr. seemed to summon up the same courage that won his father so many victories and endeared him to millions. On this night Dale Earnhardt Jr. would not be denied. He darted through the heavy traffic and overtook the first position only to be followed by an equally aggressive Michael Waltrip who would return the favor Junior's father had given him five months ago.

I do not remember shedding a tear at a sporting event since I played Little League baseball, yet the tears flowed from the eyes of what seemed like every fan in attendance, including myself.

Dale Earnhardt Jr. roared across the finish line as the champion in a performance that was as much a credit to his skills and crew as it was a tribute to his namesake.

Nothing can replace the loss of The Intimidator, the sport's fallen hero, but on this night we all were treated to a view of the strength and courage of a true NASCAR champion.

Like father, like son.

Matthew E. Adams

Our Own Perfect Rainbow

I have set my rainbow in the clouds, and it will be the sign of the covenant between me and the Earth.

Genesis 9:13

Just when I thought there could be no way to comfort my two precious children, Robbie and Krista, only hours after burying their father, Davey, God delivered a special gift just for us.

The morning was cloudy and overcast with light drizzles, on and off. The funeral was behind us now. The only thought that raced through my mind was how to console my fragile children after all they had been through over the past few days.

My home was filled with close family and friends as we all tried to take care of each other at such an emotional time. Robbie and Krista were priority for everyone in the house.

My father had taken the children to play in the back-yard to give them a break from the chaos inside the house.

As each group of friends would leave, I would walk them to the front door to see them off. This particular time, we all walked out the front door to find the most amazing sight: The end of a rainbow was clearly in our front yard. We were astonished, to say the least.

Before I could catch my breath, my father and the children were calling from the backyard to come look at the beautiful rainbow in the backyard.

It couldn't be. I ran to the backyard to see that, indeed, the other end of the rainbow was in our backyard. I looked over the house to see the most perfect rainbow shooting its colors directly over our house—a complete, perfect rainbow right in front of our eyes.

There were no words to describe the warmth in my heart for what we were witnessing: a true gift from God. It was a sign to me that he was with us and that he was giving us his promise of the covenant between God and Earth.

As I tucked Robbie and Krista into their beds that night, Krista asked if her daddy sent that rainbow to her and Robbie. I couldn't help but think he had a little something to do with it.

We then thanked God for our own perfect rainbow.

Liz Allison

An Organization with Heart

Driving past a car-repair shop in Florida, I saw a large black car that had the #3 on its side. It was parked next to the road. Around it a large crowd had gathered, getting pictures taken in front or gazing inside.

Recognizing the markings of a NASCAR vehicle, I asked my husband if he knew whose car that was. The moment he saw that black beauty, he turned ours around and headed to the shop. "Wow, that's Dale Earnhardt's car!"

Louis, my husband, sounded very excited about seeing the vehicle. While he parked our car, I noticed that the shop was having a charity to benefit handicapped kids. There were several kids in wheelchairs sitting behind a table with donation buckets.

"Hi," one said. "Are you here to see Dale's car?"

I smiled, "My husband is."

"Is Earnhardt here?" my husband asked a boy missing one foot.

"No," the kid said, "but you can see the #3, even look inside."

My husband immediately pulled me into the crowd. Around the black car several large men loomed like security guards. I could barely believe that a car would have security!

"Don't touch it," one man grumbled as my husband leaned in the window.

"No problem," Louis stuck his head in and pulled me closer. "Look!"

I slowly moved in and peered into the car. My first impression was that it wasn't anything like a normal car inside. It had large posts protecting the driver's seat, and the dash almost looked like something out of the fifties. Nothing fancy, it didn't even have windows—only mesh.

"That's nice," I said.

"Isn't this amazing? This car can go hundreds of miles an hour," my husband praised.

"Would you like to get your picture taken?" another child in a wheelchair asked, holding a Polaroid camera.

"Sure," my husband said. I turned around as he snapped a picture. The moment the picture shot out, not quite developed yet, my husband asked, "How much do I owe you?"

"Nothing, it's free."

"Next," the security guard said.

My husband and I backed away from the car and let others stand in our place. Walking back to our vehicle, my husband dropped a ten-dollar bill into one of the donation buckets on the table.

The child missing a foot smiled. "Thank you for coming to our benefit."

Driving away, I saw the smile on my husband's face and the awe in his eyes. Impressed, I had to admit to myself that I, too, was touched by this experience. I had just seen a car raise money for kids!

That same year Dale Earnhardt died in a tragic crash, but I never forgot the fact that I saw his #3 at that benefit. I grew to respect NASCAR on that day. There's more to this sport than fast cars and fearless drivers; it's about an organization with heart. NASCAR does whatever it can to help its fans, including sending a car to raise money for handicapped kids.

Michele Wallace Campanelli

My Visit to Ground Zero

*Last, but by no means least, courage—moral
courage, the courage of one's convictions, the
courage to see things through. The world is in a
constant conspiracy against the brave. It's the
age-old struggle—the roar of the crowd on one
side and the voice of your conscience on the other.*

Douglas MacArthur

When I drove the No. 31 Richard Childress Racing (RCR)
Chevrolet across the finish line and took the checkered
flag that November at New Hampshire International
Speedway, I had never before experienced so many mixed
emotions about such a long-awaited moment in my life. It
was supposed to be one of the best days of my life, but I
couldn't enjoy it as I'd always dreamed of. After trying on
and off for ten years, I had finally won my first NASCAR
Winston Cup race—and with a team I had committed to
driving for the following year.

But in the same second, the reason we were racing at
Loudon on November 23 instead of September 16 hit me
like a ton of bricks. Almost three thousand innocent

Americans had lost their lives September 11. So during the victory lap at Loudon, my car owner Richard Childress, the No. 31 team members and I decided over the team radio to donate all of our winnings from that race to the Uniformed Firefighters Association's Widows' and Children's Fund. That was the least we could do. Thousands of Americans had no reason to celebrate that Thanksgiving weekend.

After the post-race flurry had settled down a bit in Welcome, North Carolina, at the Richard Childress Racing shop, we put our heads together and came up with how we wanted to present our Loudon winnings to the fund. Richard and I thought that it would be pretty cool to hand over the check at the Waldorf-Astoria in New York City at the beginning of the festivities for the NASCAR Winston Cup banquet. Several firefighters were already invited to New York for the banquet as special guests of NASCAR and Winston. Everyone at RCR worked really hard that next week to make that happen, and the next thing I knew we were on the RCR plane headed for New York on Thursday, November 29.

We took off from the RCR hangar in Lexington, North Carolina that morning and flew into Teterboro Airport in New Jersey. From there, we were driven to the Waldorf-Astoria, where everyone had gathered in the Park South room of the hotel for the check presentation. In a very quick but meaningful ceremony, Richard and I presented the check for $203,924 to the Uniformed Firefighters Association's Widows' and Children's Fund. The only reason we raced that weekend was because of the tragedy that happened on September 11. The firefighters of New York City and their families had been through so much, and Richard, the team and I just wanted to do something to say "thank you" and let them know that everyone at RCR was still thinking about them.

That's the part of the day that most people saw. But my day in New York was just beginning. After the check presentation was complete, the guys representing the firefighters let me drive the fire truck from the Waldorf-Astoria to the midtown Manhattan high-rise firehouse that houses Engine 8, Ladder 2 and Battalion 8. I guess they figured I couldn't cause too much trouble since the firehouse was located only a couple of blocks away from the hotel.

The firefighters welcomed me just as family would, introduced me to everyone and offered me lunch. Those guys were all very cool, down-to-earth people, especially considering what they had been through and were still suffering with each and every day. I probably enjoyed that part of the trip more than any other because it was nice having close, personal time with the firefighters. They truly are heroes.

After lunch, they gave me another shot at driving the fire truck. We had the sirens blaring and the lights flashing and pulled up right in front of the Park Place entrance to the hotel. I found Rick Sanders, then president of R. J. Reynolds's Sports Marketing Enterprises, and went to hail a cab for Ground Zero. But we found out the ride was going to take too long to get down there, so we wandered back to the firehouse to see if we could bum a ride with those guys. But everyone was out on a call, so I got an idea. Without telling anyone what I was doing, I snuck over next door to the police station to look for a ride to Ground Zero. Sure enough, I found someone to take us, and we piled in a police van.

The police officer was great and got us downtown in no time. He turned on the flashing lights and the siren occasionally, and a street officer stopped traffic at an intersection to allow us to drive the wrong way down a one-way street. The trip down there was pretty exciting, but when we arrived at Ground Zero, the excitement quickly diminished and the mood grew darker.

What I would soon see was something none of us could ever imagine witnessing in our worst nightmares. We met the guys from the crane company, who gave us hard hats and credentials to permit us into the restricted work area. By that time, the weather had taken on the same characteristics as our moods: dark, drizzly and misty. When I could finally get up close and take everything in at Ground Zero, I was absolutely overwhelmed at the total destruction in front of my eyes. All the television cameras and still photographs in the world couldn't do the scene justice. It was an absolute disaster. It still smelled like smoke, and there was ash and debris as far as I could see.

They took us on the tour of Ground Zero and into the pit. I talked to the guys who had given hundreds and hundreds of hours of their time to the cleanup effort and took photos with them. What an incredibly hard job they had, but yet they never quit, despite everything that they were going through emotionally and physically.

Anyone who knows me knows that I am a hands-on guy who doesn't like to sit around and watch stuff happen around me. I've got to be right in the middle of everything. With that said, I talked my way into the cab of one of the excavating cranes and was allowed to operate the boom, although there was nothing on the hook. We spent about an hour at Ground Zero, thanked everyone who showed us around and piled back into the police van for the ride back to the Waldorf. I got to keep my hard hat, which was pretty special to me.

I was scheduled to fly back to Lexington that evening, but the weather was terrible and we couldn't get out of the airport. I decided just to stay back and visit with some of the firefighters over dinner. It was very laid-back, and we cut up a lot—I hope it took their minds off what they were facing just a bit. I stopped by several of the NASCAR Winston Cup banquet parties that evening, most notably Jeff Gordon's. I guess you could say I wasn't exactly an invited guest, but I walked in nevertheless. Keep in mind this was just days after our little skirmish at Loudon. After everyone got over the initial shock of seeing me at Jeff's party, everything was cool. I congratulated him on winning the NASCAR Winston Cup championship, and we chitchatted for awhile, but I didn't stay too long because I didn't want to overstay my welcome. I went back to the hotel and tried to get some sleep. I was so wired from the day that I just laid there and reflected on what I'd seen and done.

When I boarded the plane the next morning to head back to Lexington, I realized how exhausted I was. I hadn't been that physically and emotionally worn out in a long time, but it was definitely worth it. That day in New York City at Ground Zero was probably the most worthwhile moment in my life, and I am so grateful that I had the experience of seeing it firsthand. We knew when we won the race at New Hampshire that we wanted to help out the victims of September 11, but I didn't really realize the magnitude of what and whom we were helping until I saw it myself. The relief and recovery effort is a huge testament to how strong this country is. Some countries would never have recovered from such a tragedy, much less emerged stronger. America rallied around the victims of September 11 like it never has before and showed the true integrity and heart of this great nation. All you had to do was attend a NASCAR Winston Cup race or watch one on television after September 11 to see the unity that the terrorists' actions had produced in the citizens of the United States. American flags fly everywhere now, and the national anthem is sung and played more than ever.

Although the events of September 11 will never be forgotten, the United States is recovering slowly but surely from the terror of that dark day. The healing will never stop, and some aspects of our society will forever be changed. One thing that won't change is the spirit of the American people in pulling themselves through this. I'm just thankful that I had the opportunity to witness this for myself.

Robby Gordon

A Victory That Matters

To me, the real heroes are the people who do worthwhile things without the thought of monetary gain.

Benny Parsons

Six-year-old Cassie Boone was in a struggle for survival. Already a victim of cerebral palsy, life had suddenly become tougher. She rested in her hospital bed at Riley Children's Hospital in Indianapolis, Indiana, with her stomach laid open and exposed from surgery. Family and hospital staff would come to her side, but most visitors found the sight too unbearable. Even the family priest would stand in the doorway for prayer and apologize as he quickly exited into the hallway.

One day a visitor entered the room. He walked next to Cassie's bed, gently took her hand, stroked her hair and sat down by her side. His name was Jeremy Mayfield, a fresh young face on the NASCAR Winston Cup racing circuit. In town for the 1995 Brickyard 400 race, Jeremy had come to Riley Children's Hospital unannounced, without any media, to visit the children.

He asked Cassie about her family, her friends, her hobbies and her illness. Cassie was overjoyed with the attention she received from her new friend. Her smile was one that her family will always remember. Jeremy stocked up Cassie with hats and other gifts he had brought along. When he sensed Cassie growing tired, he squeezed her hand, said good-bye and left to visit another child. On that day, Jeremy Mayfield became a hero to the Boone family.

Eighteen months after Jeremy's visit, Cassie unexpectedly lost her battle for life. Although each day is difficult, her family has found comfort knowing that, for the first time, Cassie has a perfect body in heaven. They also find comfort in the fond memories Cassie left behind. One of those memories is the visit Jeremy made with Cassie. "I will never forget the joy on Cassie's face that day," said Cassie's mother, Linda. "Her smile seemed to last forever. Jeremy will always be special to our family."

Jeremy Mayfield had a breakout year in 1998. The Owensboro, Kentucky, native became one of the NASCAR Winston Cup point leaders, finishing in seventh place for the year and winning his first NASCAR Winston Cup race. He was suddenly on the cover of every NASCAR magazine. Everyone loves a winner, and on the track Jeremy had become a winner. But to the Boone family, and to the other children at Riley Hospital on a hot summer day in 1995, Jeremy Mayfield showed that he was already a winner. To touch the heart of a child, to bring a smile through the pain, to bring a ray of hope in a life of defeat, to give a family a memory that will always bring joy . . . that is a victory that matters.

Brad Winters

A Mother's Mission

"Your son is going blind. He has retinitis pigmentosa, and there is no cure."

I clutched my four-your-old. "How many years does he have?" I asked.

The doctor left. My question was also left unanswered, mostly because with retinitis pigmentosa, there are no clear answers. It is a rare eye disease that affects approximately 100,000 to 200,000 Americans. There is no proven treatment—no cure.

It was a hard pill to swallow. Although I could accept this fate and prepare my son for a life of darkness, I refused to accept it sitting down. My family began a mission to raise awareness of this strange and unheard-of disease. With heightened awareness comes a cure. Somebody, some company, some rich person, or maybe several thousand people could band together and raise funds until hundreds of thousands of dollars are accumulated. A small price to pay for sight. Somehow, I had to get that revenue to the Foundation Fighting Blindness.

I did the only thing I knew to do—I took Colton's story to the public. I figured raising public awareness was the cornerstone in finding a cure. In no time, my son had several front-page articles in the *Bakersfield Californian*, then many stories on NBC-TV. People from all over the world mailed Colton cards, pictures and lovely letters. But of all people, perhaps the ones who reached out the most, were the ones in the NASCAR community. I am not speaking of just one driver, but many. Colton's misfortune helped build a bridge between the drivers and fans of NASCAR, urging them to join hands to help my little boy.

NASCAR's relationship with Colton began in the fall of 2001, with a 6 A.M. phone call. The caller identified himself as George Sweat, technical representative with DuPont. He explained that he had followed Colton's NBC-TV stories and was eager to bring Jeff Gordon's showcar to show my son. George wanted to be a part of "showing the world" to him. Well, not only did he and his crew share the car with Colton, but also the other 900-plus children from his school. Colton was so excited as he rode around the parking lot!

Months later, in the spring of 2002, we met with both Jeff and Jimmie Johnson in Fontana, California, where Jeff unselfishly gave his time to our family. There were no media present, just Jeff, being wonderful to yet another hurting child.

We created our own Web site—*www.caringbridge.org/ca/coltonmeyer*. In a few short weeks, we had thousands of hits and hundreds of supportive messages, most of them from the huge NASCAR family. The fans of Jeff Gordon, Steve Park, Dale Earnhardt Jr. and many others took to Colton and his plight.

Among Colton's strongest supporters are children themselves, rallying around one of their own and trying to help. A little girl named Dani sold lemonade at her mother's yard sale. A group of children from Texas banded together and sponsored a car wash for the Foundation Fighting Blindness.

The power of love has never ceased to amaze me. To witness how a child can command so much attention and love is a testament to the "strength of love" and the "power of unity."

Because the NASCAR community continues to pull together in helping my son and spreading his story, we just might see our family mission come true.

Laura Cleverly

A Little Further Down the Road

What lies before us and what lies behind us are tiny matters to what lies within us.

Unknown

Up until the time that I was eight or nine years old, I thought everyone's father had a race car. I didn't know that anybody did anything else. I never thought of what my father did as being different from what anybody else's father did. We just went to races on the weekends and traveled around and saw a lot of the country from the time I was in the first or second grade. We went to California, New York, Florida and a little bit of everywhere.

We used to go up and down the highway in station wagons or regular passenger cars. This was long before the minivans or big vans were around. It was nothing for us to leave on a Thursday afternoon and drive straight through to Michigan, which could take fifteen or sixteen hours. If you say, "Okay, how can families be close together?" I say, "Just lock them in a car and make them ride around for sixteen hours, and they'll be close." My sisters Sharon and Lisa had their own little world, playing with Barbies; I'd be in the back with a baseball glove, and we'd all be talking together. I think that's why we are such a close family now. We talk almost every day.

When anything new came along on a car, like electric windows or lights in the back, we'd run the battery down. There's nothing my father hated worse than to come out after a race and the battery be dead in the car. On one of our trips to Michigan, a fuse blew, and we got locked in the car because we couldn't get the automatic door locks to open. My mother pulled up at a Chrysler dealership, and the salesman came out to find this woman with three kids in a car screaming through the window because the window wouldn't roll down, either.

We grew up next door to my grandfather in a small farming community called Level Cross where everybody knew you. The guy down the road was a dairy farmer and in the other direction was a tobacco farmer. To them my father wasn't Richard Petty; he was just Richard, and my grandfather was just Lee.

The family farms around here have been here for seventy-five or a hundred years. I always compare our racing business to a family farm. For us, our farm was the race cars; we have cars instead of crops. This has always been a family endeavor. When my grandfather started, it wasn't about going out and winning the trophies; it was about putting food on the table for your family. It was about survival when they started, but this is all we know, and it is all we do.

There are times when the family connection hasn't been the best thing, and we've suffered tragedy because of it. From the time my father started dating my mother, her only brother, Randy, helped in the business. Uncle Randy thought Richard Petty hung the moon. He was only five years older than me and was more like a brother than an uncle. To my father, he was like a son. Randy always wanted to work on race cars and helped Dad during the summers of his junior-high and high-school years, then full-time after high school. He had been working for a couple of years when a pit-road accident happened in Talladega. An air tank or water tank blew up and killed him. After the accident, Dad had to come back and be with my mother and my grandparents, and that was very hard for the family to get through.

I started hanging out around the business when I was twelve. From the time I was in the third grade, I went all summer long with the race team. As soon as baseball season was over, right after school was out, I would travel with my father. In my senior year of high school I told my father I wanted to drive and race. He told me I had to wait until I was twenty-one. He said, "Well, you know your mother and I really want you to go off to college." I told him, "Just let me try it and if I don't like it, then I'll go to college." That was the kicker because I think he knew I was going to like it, and he knew I'd never go to college. My mother wanted me to be a pharmacist. I can't imagine myself being a pharmacist.

I ran my first race when I was only eighteen years old. It was the ARCA race at Daytona. I had no experience, just really good people working with me, and I don't remember a lot about it. They gave me a car and said, "Go run 195 miles an hour." I was fortunate and won the race. When I look back on it, it was just a lot of fun, but it wasn't my job. My job was still working on the pit crew and working for my father. I drove his car one weekend and won a race, and then as soon as Monday came around, I was back at the racetrack working on his car and doing other things with him.

I met my wife, Patty, through my sister, Sharon, and their horse shows. Patty worked for Winston, and she was one of the R. J. Reynolds girls. We dated for a couple of years and then married in '79. She didn't grow up around racing. Her father worked a regular nine-to-five job and had weekends off and took normal vacations. I think it was hard on her in the beginning, but gradually she's gotten used to the racing lifestyle. That was twenty-two years ago, and we still have horses. Now I have a daughter, Montgomery Lee, who shares Patty's love of horses.

Our son Austin has always loved kids, even when he was still a kid. As he got a little older, he started spending time at camps and doing things with church organizations. When he was sixteen, he joined a mission group that went to Romania to build playgrounds and orphanages. For the past four years, he has been a camp counselor for critically ill children with AIDS, cancer or hemophilia.

I did with Adam what my father did with me—I neither encouraged nor discouraged him from pursuing racing as a career. I have steered Austin and Montgomery Lee in the same way. I tell them, "One day, you're going to wake up and decide what you want to do and what you want to be. When you're sure in your heart of hearts that's what you want to do, I'll help you any way I can."

Adam started by running go-carts, then he wanted a late-model stock car. So we bought it and I told him, "You put it together, we'll work on it, and we'll go racin'." We worked on it for about three weeks, and then he didn't show up anymore. About six or seven months went by, and one day he came back and said, "I think I'm ready to put that thing together now." We went back and worked. He was ready.

After Adam's death, our family sat down and talked about who would drive the #45 car. It has been a healing process for me to drive it, to get back in the car and feel that connection, that closeness. Going to the shop and seeing those guys working on the car has been a part of the healing process for our family.

Patty and I have always spent a lot of time with our children. One important thing we've done from the beginning is to live in small houses. We never had a big house. Everybody's room was right there together. Even today, Montgomery Lee and Austin's rooms are right above us so that when they get out of bed in the middle of the night, you can hear them and you know where they are and they know where you are.

Every night before we go to bed, we all gather in our room and say prayers, and we always have. From the time that Adam was born, and from the time that each one was old enough to walk and talk and understand what prayer was, we have prayed together. Even with the recent tragedy of Adam's death, Montgomery Lee and Austin still come in, and we all get together and say prayers before we all divide up and go to our own rooms. Austin may be gone to a movie until eleven-thirty or twelve o'clock at night, but when he comes in we get together, even if it's only for five or six minutes.

I've always wanted to be a part of everything my kids did. During the years my grandfather was raising a family, his main focus was keeping his family alive. He was molded and shaped by being born in the early 1900s and coming through the depression and two world wars. Society taught men that you go off to war, you fight, you come back and you don't talk about what you saw. There was no such thing as being "shell-shocked" and having "syndromes." Guys just came back and picked up and were basically expected to carry on from where they left off. My father came along and was molded, to some degree, by the changes in America during the '50s and '60s during the time of Vietnam and the civil unrest. His focus, too, was on putting food on the table for his family. When I was born, Vietnam went on, but as a nine-year-old, I paid no attention to the war. I had the luxury of being able to relate to my family in a different way than my grandfather or father could.

It's easier for fathers to show emotions to their little girls than to their sons. I can't imagine not kissing Montgomery Lee or telling her I love her every time she walks out the door. At the same time, I think that's what you should do with your sons, too. Austin never leaves on a date, never goes to bed, never hangs up the phone without me telling him I love him. Adam never got into a race car that I didn't kiss him and say a prayer and tell him I loved him. He never walked out the door or hung up the phone that I didn't tell him. The last time I talked to Adam, Montgomery Lee and I were on an airplane flying to England, and we called him from the air. We both told him we loved him. There's not a doubt in my mind he knew that when the accident happened. I think that the most important thing in life is to tell your kids because they know they are loved, and then they'll pass that love along to somebody else.

When I look back on the forty years I've been alive and the things that have happened in my life, there are only really two or three defining moments that changed the course of my life. The first one was when my Uncle Randy was killed when I was only fourteen. I realized that you couldn't just take the hands of the clock and click it back and rearrange events to make it not happen. At the same time, in the same hour, I realized that I needed Christ as a personal Savior because there was more than just being here on Earth and doing what we do. Adam's accident was another defining moment. You begin to question what is important. Winning races and all the other stuff isn't important. Montgomery Lee's important, Patty's important, Austin's important, and my relationship with Christ is important. Helping other people and making people's lives better or happier is important. We refocused on that sort of thing after the accident, supporting the Starbright Foundation that Adam had been a part of and several other children's charities.

It has definitely refocused me and my Christianity. To say that God gave his only son, you can't imagine how hard that was. I've got two sons; I had Adam, and I've got Austin. One of my sons is gone. I can't imagine how hard it was that his only son was sent to save all of us. It would be an incredible sacrifice for a human, much less for a God.

We are blessed that God gave us life, and we should go through life loving it, enjoying it and making the most out of every day. We should try to help somebody along the way, too. There is a great saying I've heard that goes, "You never help somebody climb the hill without getting a little bit closer to the top yourself." I think that's the way it is. As we go through life, if we can help somebody along, the first thing you know, we're a little further down that road, too.

Kyle Petty

Preparing for the Ultimate Healing

I really don't have goals to be the greatest coach in the business. I just try to achieve the best with the talent God has given me. If I do that, I'm satisfied.

Tom Landry

The sun warmed the April morning air that felt fresh and crisp against my face as I walked from the parking lot to the rocking chair–lined front porch of the familiar Cracker Barrel restaurant at Exit 36. I come here every Tuesday morning at eight, going immediately to the round table that sits alone in a corner just as you enter the dining area. It is here at this table that a small group meets each week to discuss some of life's most important issues. It is so routine that I can predict each week the arrival of each person and what they do and where they will sit. Ronnie Stevens, a businessman connected with racing, has been at the table for probably half an hour already, reading the newspaper and having a cup of coffee. I arrive next and join him, sitting to his right. Moments later, Michael Waltrip, a NASCAR race driver, and his dad,

Leroy, will enter. Michael sits to my right, and Leroy heads to the men's room before seating himself next to Ronnie. Moments later, Buffy, Michael's wife, and Dana, Michael's niece, arrive to fill in the remaining seats at the table.

This Tuesday morning was just different. I knew that Ronnie would not be there. I sat on the long, narrow front porch in one of the many rocking chairs, enjoying the morning sun as it beamed directly on me. It was a wonderful morning in all its glory. I sat, waiting for the others to arrive. Much to my amazement, Leroy drove up all by himself. I was really surprised, as Leroy had all but given up on driving and the others in the family would not let him drive. I figured that he must have sneaked off without the others knowing about his driving to the Cracker Barrel that morning.

"Good morning," Leroy greeted me with a sheepish smile. "Michael is out of town, and Buffy and Dana can't come this morning, so I just drove myself down today. I guess it's just you and me." We walked in together to our usual round table in the corner. In our life-issue studies, we had been discussing some things about life after death. After we made our usual order and said our "Howdy"s to the waitress, Leroy spoke out quickly about what was on his mind. "You know, I've got lots of questions about this dying thing. Max, you have been my teacher. I need to know how to get through with this dying thing. I want to know all I can about what the Bible says about dying, about heaven. I just have lots of questions." I was sensitive to Leroy's need, knowing that he had been battling cancer for some time. We began to discuss the reality of death and the hope of eternal life with God. We talked about his fears. Even though it was just the two of us, this meeting changed the setting for the group discussions for the next eight months.

Tuesdays became a more meaningful experience to the group, as we all joined in with helping Leroy prepare for death. We talked about fears of the unknown, comparisons of birth and death, life after death, and, most of all, preparations. It was a time that we all looked forward to with great anticipation as we engaged with Leroy in the planning of his departure and the discovery that death for a believer in Christ is really ultimate healing. One day Leroy asked, "Max, will you help me plan my funeral? I don't want a lot of crying. I want it to be happy." I sat with him to outline the service that some day would come. He was pleased with our plans.

Tuesday, January 11, was the crowning day of all our meetings. Early that morning I caught a plane from West Palm Beach, Florida, to rush to the Cracker Barrel gathering. I knew that Leroy would not be at this meeting. He had been hospitalized and returned home much too weak for the trip to Exit 36. I had tried to reach Michael on Monday to see if we could meet with Leroy at the house instead. Upon my arrival in Charlotte, Missy, my executive assistant, called me to say that Michael had just called to report that Leroy had had a bad night and was not doing well. Before I could call Michael, he called and said that Leroy had quietly slipped into the presence of God. He died peacefully, knowing that all was well with God. He had given evidence of that throughout our meetings.

Wednesday, January 12, we gathered at the First Baptist Church of Mooresville, North Carolina, to celebrate Leroy's life and his crowning day. With two popular drivers in the family, the church was filled with family, friends and those from the racing community. Leroy had been a part of the NASCAR scene since Darrell's entry into the sport in the mid-1970s. The memorial service was very different. It literally was a happy occasion. It was carried out just as Leroy had planned. Darrell shared some fond memories of his dad. Ronnie Stevens talked about the Tuesday meetings at the Cracker Barrel. Michael spoke of Leroy's fifty years of marriage to Margaret, his love of golf, his dressing like a man in *GQ* and his love for God. He shared this quote from C. S. Lewis: "If I cannot find the things in this world that will fulfill my deepest longings, then perhaps I am made for a different world."

Leroy entered that different world—a world without sickness or pain. We all joined in the celebration of Leroy's ultimate healing. People left that day different because Leroy's plans gave cause for celebration and a different view of dying.

Max Helton

5

FOR THE LOVE OF NASCAR®

There's more to this sport than fast cars and fearless drivers; it's about an organization with heart.

Michele Wallace Campanelli

Teamwork Works

Individuals play the game, but teams win championships.

Sign in New England Patriots' locker room

Webster defines a team as marked by devotion to teamwork. It was made clear on a Saturday night during the 2001 NASCAR Winston Cup season that teamwork is crucial to the entertainment we watch every week. In short, pit crews are important. It is nothing short of amazing that we can name a driver, his wife, his number, his paint scheme, his sponsor, his crew chief, his hometown and possibly even his birthday. Yet we can't name his catch can man.

On the first lap of The Winston, heavy rain fell on Lowe's Motor Speedway, and Kevin Harvick, Jeff Gordon, Jeff Burton and Michael Waltrip all ended up with wrecked race cars. It appeared that their night was over. However, because The Winston is a non-points event, special rules apply to this race that do not apply to regular races. Because of one clause in the NASCAR rule book, all four drivers were allowed to bring out their back-up cars. To be competitive, Jeff Burton knew a different engine would have to be installed in his #99 Citgo Ford. That began the thrashing in the garage area.

It might be said that if Jeff Burton's crew had not worked so hard on installing that new engine that they would never draw a check from Roush Racing again. But that wasn't said. No, anyone could see that these men believed in their driver and that their driver believed in them. They worked feverishly as sweat and stress became evident on their faces. One might expect that only Jeff Burton's crewmembers would be around his car. Instead it was a collage of color with people from all cars of Roush Racing and even Ed Wood of the Wood Brothers. They were all working tirelessly on a car that might turn out to be the one to defeat them when the night was over. It didn't matter, what mattered was getting the #99 back on the track to represent the hopes and dreams of all who built her.

FOX flashed an engine change clock on the bottom of the screen while their cameras zoomed in on the efforts taking place in the garage. The minutes began ticking by and the men kept working. While Jeff Burton's crew was changing the engine, the crews of Jeff Gordon, Kevin Harvick and Michael Waltrip were trying to zero in on the setup that would win the race. They were shooting blindly in the dark to guess what would work. Their best guess on the setup evaporated when their primary cars hit the wall on lap 1. Yes, Jeff Gordon was correct when he said it would make a good story.

However, sometimes the story is not in the winner. Sometimes the story is not in the fireworks, the money or the flashbulbs. Instead, the story is in Jeff Burton's crew. The story is in every crew who works every week to make it possible for our favorite cars to crank it up. They have the power to bring in a simple chassis and make it the winning car. It's a combination of determination, heart, intelligence, patience and, most of all, teamwork.

Yes, it might be a good thing to pay attention to that catch can man next time you see him. But then again, there are always those who stand in the shadows to give another some time in the sunshine.

Jenni Thompson

Smokey

The last time I spoke with Smokey Yunick, it was by phone. Heard his health had been deteriorating, and wanted to check up on him.

"I've never been dead before, so I don't know what it's like," he said. "I could be dead right now and not know it."

In his typical sailor talk that belied an otherwise brilliant mind, Smokey suggested his problem lately had been a lack of "romance."

We'd eventually find out it was leukemia that would claim Smokey in the shallow hours of a Wednesday morning. While he would never go into much detail about his ailments and his odds of beating them, he remained typically blunt about the overall picture.

He loved the laughter that would greet such statements. When people—fans, reporters, whoever—would meet Smokey for the first time, they'd bring with them the belief they were meeting a genius, and in many ways, they were. In automotive circles, from the engineering labs in Detroit to the garage stalls of Darlington, Smokey was held up as a mechanical god worthy of Mount Rushmore.

Gearheads from all corners of the globe, when visiting this area, would often drop by "The Best Damn Garage in

Town" on North Beach Street, if not for an actual visit, then just to snap a picture of the shop. That sprawling garage, for many people, was to automotive development what Memphis' Sun Records was to rock 'n' roll.

But within two minutes of beginning a conversation with Smokey, a stranger would suddenly find his ears filling with the type of language usually reserved for pool halls and poker tables. You'd have to laugh at the absurdity of it all, this man who was able to decorate talk of physics and combustion with a string of R-rated ornaments. It was, in a strange way, artistic.

Smokey would smile at the surprised look on a stranger's face and then continue his lesson. Quite often, when asked to explain a certain topic, he'd begin with, "Now, you probably don't know this, but. . . ."

There was a lot he knew and a lot we didn't. And if you had the time, he'd walk you through a lesson on the wide range of his specialties, from hydraulics and power steering to fuel economy and ignitions. And he'd gladly share his opinions on everything, even the evils of cruise control.

"So many of these highway wrecks are caused by someone falling asleep at the wheel," he said. "And most of these people probably had their cruise control on. I'd say, 'Wake up, fella. You're about to miss one whale of a wreck.'"

But for all his work in general automotive mechanics work and research that affects you every time you drive to the corner store, Smokey might've never become a mechanical household name if not for automobile racing.

Back in racing's caveman days, the 1950s and '60s, when mechanics had more rulebook leeway in which to play, Smokey was truly in his element. The small-block engine, which Smokey massaged for racing purposes during its original mid-1950s' development, was like a blank canvas awaiting an artist's imagination and touch, and Smokey could paint a winner.

Smokey built cars from the ground up and would win races and/or championships with the likes of drivers Herb Thomas, Fireball Roberts and Curtis Turner.

It was a time when the men involved would work like dogs all day and part of the night, often supplementing their meager nutritional intake with pulls from something contained in a brown bag. They'd spend what remained of the evening trying to charm the local female population, and then start anew the next dawn.

But it was an era when Big Bill France was wining and dining the big automakers from Detroit, trying to get them interested in NASCAR. This schmoozing, many old-timers will tell you, would often include on-track favors, and after feeling like the victim of certain political moves too many times, Smokey left NASCAR for good in 1970.

"In 1970," Smokey recalled a few years ago, "when I left, I said, 'France, this is the end of it. I ain't never gonna (mess) with you again, you rotten no-good (SOB). I'm gone.' He said, 'You'll be back.' I said to him, 'France, if you don't think I'm gone, you count the days until I come back.' I would've never, ever gone back."

Five years later, after nearly two decades of building Indy cars and hauling them to Indianapolis each May, Smokey also gave up his open-wheel efforts when he tired of the modernization of that game. And that one hurt, because he truly loved Indianapolis and what it represented.

"Back in the old days, I would've pulled my car in Indianapolis with a rope if I had to," he said. "That was the ultimate, to stand there on the starting grid on race day at the Indianapolis 500 and pull up your pants and say, 'Okay, you mothers, let's have a race.'"

Though his efforts no longer showed up on the sports pages, he still found great thrill in his backroom work at the Beach Street garage. He loved learning new things as much as he loved inventing new things. And anyone who ever visited him at that dusty shop and sat inside that cold, dark office will miss the pleasure that came from visiting a man who, well into his seventies, still knew his stuff and took great pleasure in enlightening others.

Before hanging up with Smokey a couple of months back, I warned him that I'd be making another one of those visits someday soon.

"Don't wait too long," he warned back, knowing the ominous threat would draw a chuckle.

But we always wait too long. Thankfully, though, Smokey was one of the lucky ones—his work in this world will be felt and remembered for a long time.

Ken Willis

The Day I Will Never Forget

Thinking back, February 18, 2001, was a gorgeous day. Sunshine filled the sky, and as I entered the garage area at Daytona International Speedway I could swear I felt droplets of God's grace hit me in the face at every step.

I couldn't help but smile. Everyone smiled. It was Sunday and time for the greatest spectacle in NASCAR. It was the Daytona 500, and man, it was a good day to be alive.

Slight bits and pieces from that day occupy my memory. I remember Stone Temple Pilots blaring through my speakers. I remember needing to shave. I remember Elliot Sadler stuffing cupcakes into his mouth and Bobby Labonte making fun of my outfit at the driver's meeting. I remember Eddie Wood's sly grin when the engines were cranked. He'd been doing this for forty-five years, and it still got him fired up.

I remember watching television and smiling as Dale Earnhardt hugged his wife and namesake, whispering to each with obvious sincerity. I remember that being especially poignant at the time. It was something I hadn't seen before.

I remember wanting to explode with pride as O-Town belted out "... and the home of the brave." I remember the

cars rolling off pit road and the deafening roar that
ensued. Obviously, these fans felt fortunate to be associated with such a marquee event.

I felt the same way; everyone did. Life on the road can
make you quite jaded, but not at Daytona, not on the
most celebrated day in motorsports. You're happy to be at
Daytona.

From the time the cars rolled off the pit lane, it's all a bit
of a blur. I remember standing on the pit road for the
longest time, hanging out in Dale Jr.'s pit while listening
to my boy Brett Griffin in his debut as Sadler's spotter. At
the outset, the race was a bit monotonous.

It was awesome, don't get me wrong, but not the most
exciting event I'd ever seen. Then with twenty-seven laps
to go, everything changed. Robby Gordon tapped Ward
Burton in the rear, triggering a nineteen-car pileup that
sent Tony Stewart flipping wildly through the air.

Stewart did a complete vertical flip and landed square
on Gordon's roof, barrel-rolled a few times and came to
rest on top of Labonte's roof. Everyone gasped. The accident looked horrific, but proved virtually harmless.

I remember running to the garage and seeing my
buddy Josh Neelon, Bobby Labonte's business manager,
and how livid he was at what had happened. I remember
the two of us discussing the potential for disaster that had
just been averted. I remember taking a deep breath and
saying a small prayer.

Suddenly, everyone realized that the race had evolved
in such a manner that the impossible lay right on the hori-
zon. Michael Waltrip could very well win this thing. No
way, that wouldn't happen.

He hadn't won in 462 tries. Ten laps to go: still leading,
Dale Jr. in tow. Five laps to go: still leading. White flag: still
leading. As they entered turn 2, I remember fifty media
types crammed in the corners of the media center—where

the TVs are located—nervous that somehow Mikey would blow it.

He didn't. He took the checkers just ahead of Lil E. Meanwhile, a few hundred yards back, Earnhardt had shot up the track and into the turn 4 wall. I remember Darrell Waltrip cheering for Mikey and asking about Big E at the same time.

I remember sprinting to pit road to talk to Rusty Wallace and being intersected by a friend who informed me that Big E was in bad shape. I remember seeing NASCAR Vice President George Pyne in Victory Lane and the look on his face when I told him Earnhardt was being cut out of the car. He ran to the Winston Cup hauler. I ran to the media center.

That's where I found my co-worker, Dave Rodman, typing furiously on his keyboard. I didn't want to look; I knew what he was writing. His eyes were welled up with tears. I remember him turning to me, putting his head on my shoulder and sobbing uncontrollably. He knew, and he wasn't alone.

Mike Mulhern, a decades-long motorsports journalist for *The Winston-Salem Journal,* is a gruff man, a celebrated Vietnam veteran whose unique view of the state of NASCAR—and life in general, for that matter—makes him seem like a hard-ass.

He's not. I love the guy, always have, but for the longest time I assumed he was incapable of showing emotion. Why? I don't know. I don't know him all that well, but he just seemed like a non-emotional guy.

Then Mike Helton announced that Earnhardt had died in that turn 4 crash. As Mulhern typed his obit for the Monday morning paper, he sobbed. And sobbed. And sobbed. Somehow, amidst all the frenzied thoughts, sounds and sights that raced through my head that tragic evening, that one sits at the forefront of my memory.

I remember thinking that just two hours ago, I couldn't have been happier. I was ecstatic with glee for Mikey. Now I couldn't have been sadder. I walked outside, dazed and confused. What I saw was surreal. Everyone was silent, eyes full of tears. I walked over to my car, where my wife sat reading, waiting for me to finish.

She had no idea. I told her, and finally it hit me. The look on her face was one of unadulterated shock. I broke down. My phone rang off the hook, everyone wanting to know if it was real.

I remember one call in particular, that of my buddy Hank Parker Jr., a NASCAR Busch Series driver and one of Dale Jr.'s dearest friends. I remember how scared Hank sounded when I told him it was true. Big E was his second father, a true hero in all facets of life, someone he approached for advice about career opportunities.

Big E has long been a true hero to millions of people. The seemingly limitless tributes we've seen in all corners of the country since his death only reassure his legend. Every track has given a unique tribute. Fox Television dedicates the third lap of each race to him. Fans nationwide bring personal tributes every week. Half the cars on the highway don stickers of allegiance to our fallen hero.

Though infinitely tragic, Earnhardt's accident has produced several positive reactions. It has triggered a new union among those in the industry and those in the stands. With enhanced safety awareness, cars will be safer because of his accident. An entire state rallied together to disallow the release of Earnhardt's autopsy photos.

Still, it's such a tough pill to swallow. Earnhardt was a special breed. He was a tenacious racer, an innovative businessman, a devoted father. He embodied everything that is NASCAR. He was Big Bill France's vision for what his upstart organization would become. He garnered the adoration of millions. Every time you heard his name, the raucous applause was deafening. To me, that is amazing. I'd die to be cheered like that just once, and he got it every single day.

Marty Smith

Growing Up NASCAR®

I'm a car guy.

Ever since I was a wee squirt, I've been fascinated by automobiles. My mother had often told me that my first word was not "mama" or "dada," but "car." My grandfather, an avid car collector, probably had a lot to do with this. Every gift he ever gave me was either a toy car, a model car or a book about cars. He never read me fairy tales like other grandfathers; he read me *Car and Driver* and *Automobile Quarterly*.

His estate in Verbena, Alabama, was home to nearly fifty automobiles: Packards, Daimlers, Peugeots, Citroens, even a Goliath and a Jaguar. The latter was sadly little more than a pile of rust molecules holding hands, but he loved it. He also had a huge octagonal library filled with car books, models and die-cast miniatures, and a corner closet filled with years and years of *Car and Driver, Road and Track* and *Road Test* back issues.

It was in these magazines that I gained my first exposure to auto racing and NASCAR in particular. I read about Cale Yarborough, Richard Petty, David Pearson and a host of others, thus planting the seeds that would in later years become an obsession. For the meantime, however, adolescence was approaching fast, and it wasn't long before every thought in my head was obliterated by an intense preoccupation with the opposite sex.

When I regained consciousness some six or seven years later, my passion for cars and racing was reignited by a television program called *Close Calls*. The show featured Benny Parsons, Richard Petty, Cale Yarborough and Darrell Waltrip talking about some of the hairy situations they've made it through in their racing careers. I sat there in awe of these four "good ol' boys" who were casually describing and laughing about horrific accidents and crippling injuries. *These guys are cool,* I remember thinking. Then they rolled some of the footage. . . . Richard Petty barrel rolling at Daytona, Bobby Allison slamming the catch fence at Talladega, Cale Yarborough flipping over during a qualifying run at Daytona, Richard Petty hammering the retaining wall at Darlington, Darrell Waltrip sailing backwards into a dirt bank at Daytona. The fact that these guys could endure such wrecks and then climb back into the car was amazing to me.

It was right then that I had a personal revelation, one that changed and has continued to change the course of my life. I had always been the type of person who would walk away from something if I got hurt or there seemed to be a promise of some kind of injury or letdown. Yet these guys not only put themselves in danger, but met it head-on with faith and unshakable confidence. I realized then that I was not that kind of person, but at the same time, that I desperately wanted to be. From that point on, I strove not to take the easy road or shy away from risks, and to take risks with my eyes open and my mind engaged. My newfound confidence changed my luck with school, work and the opposite sex. My life's journey with NASCAR was under way.

I spent the next few years collecting die-cast race cars

and learning everything I could about the world of NASCAR. I saw Davey Allison win his first Daytona 500 in 1992, then miss his chance at a NASCAR Winston Cup championship nine months later. In this same year, I saw Richard Petty take his last ride in competition and Jeff Gordon take his first. We all said good-bye to Clifford Allison that year, and good-bye to Alan Kulwicki and Davey himself the next year. The following year we lost Neil Bonnett. I saw John Andretti, Sterling Marlin, Jeff and Ward Burton, Jimmy Spencer, Jeremy Mayfield, Bobby Hamilton, Dale Earnhardt Jr., Matt Keneseth, Steve Park, Jerry Nadeau, Tony Stewart, Jeff Gordon and probably some I've forgotten take their first NASCAR Winston Cup win. I've seen Dale Earnhardt turn doughnuts in the Daytona grass and Dale Jarrett and Bobby Labonte on stage in New York. I've seen careers skyrocket and careers go into the toilet. Sponsors have come and gone, teams have come and gone, and many of the races today have ".com" in the title. STP is no longer plastered on car #43, and ESPN and TNN have been replaced by FOX.

My passion for NASCAR is still very strong and goes hand-in-hand with my love of automobiles. The two complement one another. My head turns at the sight or sound of a car much the same way that many men are captivated by beautiful women. My eyes are dazzled by the flashing colors, the speed and the pageantry that is NASCAR. The rumble of a well-tuned V8 does something to me that I can't quite explain. The buzzing drone of a forty-three-car pack is a siren song, and the sound of a strong automobile running through the gears speaks to me of freedom and exhilaration.

Steve Wingate

Coming Full Circle

Abingdon, Virginia, was a place I called home for nearly twelve years. Just past the city limits sign on Lee Highway and right around the corner from the Cherokee Restaurant and Motel was the headquarters for Morgan-McClure Motorsports (MMM), a three-time Daytona 500-winning team. Much like a child who grew up watching the Pittsburgh Steelers in the 1970s, I wanted to go racing. I wanted to call racing my profession.

I was sure fate would someday waltz me into a job in the motorsports world. After all, I knew some of the people at the Morgan-McClure shops. My dad drag-raced motorcycles before he lost his leg in a highway accident. On top of that, my birthday was June 19, the anniversary of the first NASCAR Winston Cup event.

My dream shattered when my mother remarried, and we moved to Pennsylvania. I cried as I watched the passing road signs. I was leaving not only my family, friends, church and hometown, but my dream. Pennsylvania wasn't a "racing state."

I was determined more than ever to get into racing and made college plans to include a move back down south so I could be in the vicinity of teams like

Morgan-McClure and tracks like Bristol Motor Speedway. In the meantime, our family got a computer. I noticed the game "NASCAR Racing 2" by Sierra on Wal-Mart shelves. Naturally, I purchased the software title and rushed home to install it on my machine. In no time, I was running around tracks with the falsely perceived skill of real-life NASCAR Winston Cup veterans. I thought I was hot stuff. I joined an online network of players and soon met many racers from across the United States. They were a lot better than I was, but that didn't matter. I met people who were more than just computer junkies.

All of these factors led me to believe that I had the mettle to compete in a real race car. Lack of funds and lack of success in a sponsorship hunt for the Goody's Dash Series, NASCAR Touring Division, soon proved to be frustrating and, again, this teenage dreamer fell short of his goal. By now, I was desperate. Was I ever going to get a job in racing? Was I ever really going to do something I loved for my entire life? I was convinced the answer was a resounding "no."

During my sophomore year in high school, our English class required a persuasive speech as a research project. Some controversial issues on the list included gun control, the death penalty and euthanasia. There was also an option to choose your own topic. Being the individual that I am, I saw an opportunity to defend my heroes. I consulted with the teacher about researching and developing a speech on the argument of whether race-car drivers should be considered athletes, a matter close to my heart. She concurred and allowed me to pursue the topic.

As a run-through of the information, and frankly for the heck of it, I wrote an essay to accompany my speech. One of the Web sites I frequented, *RaceComm.com*, requested submissions from readers, and I figured that I had nothing to lose. I was just a sophomore in high school, so I didn't expect anything too extravagant. Honestly, it would have made my heart jump to have been acknowledged with an e-mail saying, "Thanks, but this isn't exactly what we had in mind for the site." I didn't get that. What I got was a huge surprise. After logging onto the site in the following days, I saw a headline emblazoned on the home page, "Defending Your Hero." I was in shock. There it was, my essay, on a site that had traffic in excess of 50,000 views per day. Not only that, but people were reading my work! I received numerous e-mails praising it and thanking me for such an insightful article.

It hit me that there was more to do in racing than driving the car or calling the shots. Here was opportunity staring me in the face. I shook hands with it, invited it inside, and treated it to a hot meal of cornbread and fried chicken. The myth that I needed to be down south to get involved in racing flew out the back door as this opportunity manifested itself.

Amazingly, a seemingly meaningless high-school project turned my life around. It showed me that no matter where I am, I can pursue my dreams, and the geographic location is a hindrance only if I let it be. Because of that project, I'm now working in a different site doing marketing and public-relations work for teams and drivers—and living my dream.

Tony Stevens

Mothers Deserve More than One Day

Ward and I understand that there's something bigger than racing. Racing is important, but it is not more important than your family.

Jeff Burton

Unfortunately, many people focus on Mother's Day as the best chance to make their mom feel important. It's funny how holidays work. Sure it's great to remember special people on their birthdays, our faith at Christmas or Hanukkah, and our parents on Mother's and Father's Day. But what about the special things our loved ones bring us throughout the year?

As with many auto-racing fans, I was introduced to the sport by my parents. My father was an open-wheel fanatic, attending the Indianapolis 500 every year. My stepfather was a NASCAR fan, and Charlotte—the hometown of many in the sport—is where he wanted to retire.

I was fortunate, you see. I was gifted with my mother's addiction to speed and driving ability while I inherited my father's sense of direction. Yes, he finally found his calling as the navigator for Mom when they did road rallies.

When she wasn't busy erasing the tread of an innocent set of Goodyears, my mother loved to watch auto racing. Early on she was a big A. J. Foyt fan. Foyt's fiery temper and passion for winning was what caught her eye. Coincidentally, May, the month we pay "tribute" to our mothers, is also the month when the Indianapolis Motor Speedway comes alive. Foyt owns a piece of Indy car history, winning four Indianapolis 500s. Although Foyt turned out to be a heck of a choice, Mom usually loved to cheer on the underdog. When watching NASCAR, she spent her time booing the Richard Pettys and Darrell Waltrips, legends of the sport. She preferred to cheer for the Eddie Bierschwales and Chad Littles—two drivers with many years of racing experience and *no* victories.

I lost my best friend, auto racing lost its biggest fan and the cops their most elusive target in 1994, but her memories still live on. The first race I attended after my mother's death, the 1997 NASCAR Busch Series race at Daytona, Chad Little started forty-second out of forty-five cars. As the cars were heading into turn 3, about to take the white flag signaling one lap to go, the impatience among the leaders took its toll. All heck broke loose, and all I could see was smoke and spinning cars.

Then, like a Hollywood production, Little's red and yellow #23 emerged unscathed from the chaos. As Little came to the start/finish line to take the white and yellow flags, I couldn't help but scream to my stepfather, "He's going to win, he's going to win!" The next two and a half minutes seemed like an eternity as Little followed the pace car at fifty-five miles per hour to complete the final lap of the race.

While my stepfather and I had cried a river by the time Little took his first checkered flag, I couldn't help but crack a smile. That was my sign. My sign Mom was still watching.

All of my mom's passion and love for the sport of auto racing was sent to me from above that day. I was hooked. I became a Chad Little fan in February 1995. Shortly thereafter, I got to know his family and began writing for his Web site. The experience helped me get to where I am today. I get paid to cover the sport I love. I get paid to write a story like this, a story about how much I appreciate my mother each and every day.

Thanks, Mom.

Roy Lang III

A Moment in Time

I have always been a fan of NASCAR, and both as a fan and as a part-time journalist, I find it fascinating to make note of dramatic turning points in any particular sport. For the sport of NASCAR, I feel like a dramatic turning point came in 1995.

That was the year that a fresh-faced twenty-four-year-old named Jeff Gordon shocked the NASCAR world by winning his first NASCAR Winston Cup title. In doing so he had wrestled the title away from seven-time champion Dale Earnhardt. I also felt he sent a message heard around the world of racing that he would be a force to deal with for many years to come.

I will admit that at that time I was not a Jeff Gordon fan. It all seemed to come too easy to him. My bias blinded me to the reality of the years of labor, commitment and sacrifice he undoubtedly had put into his pursuit of driving excellence. No, at that time I scoured the papers and magazines for the "Dale Earnhardt perspective" on this young upstart. The Intimidator did not disappoint me as his comments seemed to suggest that he was hardly impressed with Gordon, dubbing him "The Kid" and "Wonder Boy." I laughed out loud when Earnhardt coyly suggested during an interview that Gordon would have to toast his admirers with a glass of milk because he was too young for the traditional champagne.

I felt that Earnhardt was the antidote to the wave of popularity the young Gordon was demanding. Earnhardt's reputation as an unyielding and aggressive adversary was well earned both on and off the track. So, too, was his reputation as the vehicle that had carried NASCAR to unprecedented heights of popularity.

I wondered how two such diverse personalities could co-exist in the parochial world of NASCAR. Was this town big enough for the pure-bread Gordon and Earnhardt, the man in black?

I did not have to wait very long for an answer. It was at the post-season awards banquet where Jeff Gordon displayed his not only his good nature, but his steely resolve as well. When he offered a toast to his fierce competitor, Earnhardt, I finally began to like and admire Jeff Gordon. As I watched Gordon raise his glass for the toast, the crowd erupted in laughter. The glass was filled not with champagne . . . but milk.

Dale Earnhardt chuckled and nodded his approval, and thus the dynamics of a relationship between Gordon and Earnhardt were born, which would herald NASCAR to the forefront of American sports.

Wayne Spodnick

Racing Felt Good

Like most Americans, I was glued to the news channels day and night after the September 11 attacks, to the point where I felt like I had a personal relationship with Peter Jennings, Charlie Gibson, Diane Sawyer and the host of other reporters from CNN and MSNBC. I was sitting at my computer with the television blaring in the background on that unforgettable Tuesday morning. I turned and glanced at the TV screen and saw Charlie Gibson showing the world a picture of the first World Trade Center tower billowing with smoke and flames. I watched in horror as the second plane came across the screen and rammed into the other tower. My heart leapt up in my chest, and the air whooshed from my lungs. Trembling, I reached for the phone to call my mom. Funny how we all wish for our moms when trouble surrounds us.

Since I live in a military town, I was used to hearing planes overhead. The brick sign outside the airbase reads: "Pardon our noise, but it is the sound of Freedom." I always loved that sign—the sounds of roaring airplanes never bothered me, but instead were a comfort. The eerie silence while the planes were grounded for the two days after the WTC attack haunted me. Like many Americans, I spent that first week looking everywhere for a large American flag to hang outside my house and a smaller one to fly from my car. And like many others, I soon found out there were none to be had. So I bought materials and made my own, which my husband hung proudly on the house. When I sat down to watch the Dover race, I wondered if I would have the same enthusiasm for racing as I did before September 11. It didn't take long to find out. I cried, covered in goose bumps, as I listened to Lee Greenwood and Tanya Tucker sing the national anthem and saw the crowd waving flags while chanting, "USA! USA! USA!" I was thrilled at the start of the engines. I watched enthralled as Jeff Gordon managed to control his car through every love tap and wreck. I screamed at the top of my lungs when Rusty Wallace spun out Ricky Rudd, who managed to stay in the race and finish third just in front of Gordon. I gasped as I watched Tony Stewart get into Dale Jarrett and spin him out and into a twelfth-place finish. Satisfied that Jeff had raced his very best in spite of the odds and finished fourth, I watched with immense pride as Dale Earnhardt Jr. took the victory lap while flying the Stars and Stripes from his window. And for several hours, I didn't think about the World Trade Center or the Pentagon . . . I didn't relive the site of planes crashing into buildings . . . I didn't once turn on CNN or MSNBC for the latest updates . . . I laughed and screamed and cried tears of pride and joy.

Yes, it was good to be racing again.

Jan Bazen

Think Before You Boo

*It takes so little effort to offer encouragement—
a smile, a touch, a few well-spoken words.*

Reggie Williams, Former Cincinnati Bengals Linebacker

I went to a few races this year on the NASCAR Winston Cup tour, some NASCAR Busch Series races and several local short track races. I found myself shocked to hear all of the boos aimed at Tony Stewart. *Why boo Tony?* I thought. Then I thought, *Why boo anyone?*

As I thought about this, an incident that occurred when I was seven years old came to mind.

The year was 1978, and my dad was the defending track champion at the Waterford Speed Bowl in Connecticut. He had won many races already that year and was the favorite to win the title again. As is the case, because he was so dominant, he got booed. I remember my mom trying to tell me, "Oh, they are just jealous." And I couldn't figure out how these people, who didn't even know my dad, could hate him so much.

Then one Saturday night while leading in the race coming off of turn 4, he made contact with the car to his outside. This sent him head-on into the wall halfway between turn 4 and the flag stand. The right front corner was gone, and the wheel was stuffed up under the firewall somewhere. My sister and I raced from our seats to the fence to see if he was okay, tears already flowing. When we got there, he had undone his seatbelts and was climbing out the passenger window.

All of a sudden we heard tires screeching and realized that one car had not slowed down yet. He hit my dad's car in the passenger door as my dad was climbing out. The car slid down to the flag stand and stopped up against the wall, and my dad was thrown around inside the car. We ran down to where the car ended up and saw him climbing out again. He got out of the car and said, "I'm okay, kids," and collapsed right there. As we stood in shock, the rescue workers attended to him. This lady in the front row cheered loudly. She said insulting and hurtful things. I will never forget the feeling of shock that overcame me at that point.

Fortunately, my dad's only injuries were a broken wrist and many bruises. He was lucky that day to have survived, and we were glad our dad was okay.

Since then, no matter how much I dislike a driver, I never hope for any injuries. I also will be the first one to applaud when they climb out of the car and to thank God they are okay. It is okay to have favorite drivers and to have those you don't like. That makes the competitive nature come to life. But let's stop booing these guys. Granted, their kids probably aren't sitting next to you in the stands, but I bet they are watching on television or they can hear you from the infield. And even if they don't have children, they have feelings. These guys race because it is what they love to do. Some are better than others, some are more diplomatic than others, and some haven't quite figured out how to act around mobs of fans yet.

Whatever the case may be, they are human beings with feelings and with people who love and support them.

So the next time they introduce Tony Stewart, maybe he won't have to cringe and wonder what he has done to anger all these people. Let's be thankful for the show these guys give us and the risks they take to make us scream and shout for three to four hours each week. My booing days are over, and maybe, just maybe, yours are, too.

Rob Faiella

The Final Race

When we were growing up, because our mothers were twins, Bill Caruso and I were constant childhood companions. But later, because we lived in different states, we didn't see much of each other. One evening Bill called to say he would not be attending my daughter's wedding. It was disappointing but not surprising because I understood his reason. Racing had been Bill's never-waning, lifelong passion, and now he was anticipating and preparing his car with great excitement for his upcoming race at Lime Rock, Connecticut. As Bill spoke that night about the race, his masculine yet soft voice became spirited and alive with exhilaration that came charging across the telephone lines.

When we hung up, I smiled, remembering the days before Bill and I were old enough to have driver's licenses, and Bill was convinced he wouldn't have the attention of the opposite sex without one. This turned out not to be true because when he was fourteen years old, the girls were already vying for Bill's attention and calling him often. His lack of a car and driver's license had not discouraged their interest one bit. This was not surprising to anyone else because at this young age Bill was already handsome, charismatic and possessed many endearing qualities that remained throughout his life. His understanding, along with the compassion he felt and unselfishly extended to others, touched many lives in many different ways.

One day, a smiling Bill drove into my driveway sitting regally behind the wheel of his first sleek, dark green "Morgan"—his eyes glistening as brilliantly as his car. He was sporting a dark mustache and beard that accentuated his scintillating smile. Wearing a white helmet, with his left hand casually resting on the steering wheel, it was clear he has realized his dream!

Years later I remember that just looking at him filled me with excitement as he and his peers revved up the engines; I can still hear the deafening thunder that followed and the impassioned cheering of the crowds, and I imagined the racing hearts of the drivers equaling the cars' speed at the onset. I laughed because his happiness was mine, and I was proud of him, proud to know him, and of the childhood days and memories I was fortunate enough to share with him.

After months of hard work and endless preparation, Bill's long-awaited day finally arrived with Lime Rock seething with excitement and suspense—only this time, although he and his car were there, Bill would not be driving. Just before the race began, one car slowly moved around the track. Then, a moment of silence was observed as sadness and disbelief overwhelmed everyone present, for it was Bill's car and it carried his ashes. Not only was his death a great loss for NASCAR, but also for each person whose life Bill touched. Bill was there in spirit that day, and no one was smiling brighter when those keys turned in the ignitions with the resounding explosions of cars jumping to life. *This I know.*

Barbara A. Seitz

6

THE WINNER'S CIRCLE

There are no rest areas on the highway to success.

Steve Byrnes
host of Totally NASCAR

True Heroes

A hero is no braver than an ordinary man, but he is braver five minutes longer.

Ralph Waldo Emerson

"You're my hero."

I hear the phrase almost every time I meet with a group of fans, and while I appreciate such an accolade, in reality it is misplaced. I am a race-car driver, a father, a son, a brother and a husband. I am blessed to be a part of one of the greatest sports in America, and I am lucky to be in a position that allows me to reach out and touch the lives of others through my profession.

On September 22, 2002, I had the great pleasure to honor a true American hero. On that day my #18 Interstate Batteries Pontiac Grand Prix was adorned with red, white and blue, and painted on the hood were the immortal words of Todd Beamer whose call to action was "Let's Roll." One hundred percent of the proceeds from the sale of related merchandise benefited the Todd Beamer Foundation. When Joe Gibbs first told me that the foundation benefits children and asked me if I would be interested in helping out, I immediately jumped in.

I have often heard that the strength of the sport of NASCAR comes from its fans. It is no different with a nation, this nation, the United States of America.

The story of Todd Beamer and the other brave passengers aboard United Flight 93 still brings tears to my eyes. The flight had been hijacked. After hurried and emotional cell and in-flight phone calls to loved ones, passengers learned that jet planes loaded with their fellow American citizens had been flown into the Twin Towers of the World Trade Center and the Pentagon. Faced with the horrible reality that their plane, too, was one of the rogue planes the terrorists planned to use as a human bomb, they did something absolutely incredible. Literally, to the last moments of their lives, they exercised a great American ideal. They took a vote. With a simple, common act in the most uncommon of circumstances, this group of brave citizens validated our commitment to freedom and paid the ultimate tribute to our democracy by not allowing a terrorist force to blindly predetermine their fate. They voted to save the lives of potentially thousands of other innocent people on the ground and regain control of that plane. Sadly, their heroic efforts ended in the loss of their lives as their plane crashed into a field in rural Pennsylvania.

I was tremendously honored to be able to run the red, white and blue car with the "Let's Roll" logo on the hood. As a father of two small children, it made me feel especially good to be able to help out the Todd Beamer Foundation in this way.

To Todd Beamer and his fellow patriots and heroes on United Flight 93, I say simply, *You are my heroes!*

Bobby Labonte

Life Lessons

Life is a team sport.

Michael Waltrip

Racing is the most fulfilling and exhilarating thing that I have ever done.

Racing is a part of me, a part of who I am. I was literally born into a racing family. My brother Darrell was sixteen when I was born and already on his way to a racing career. I can remember my parents taking us down to Daytona for Speed Weeks when I was a kid. Nobody else's parents were taking them out of school to go to races. Nobody else's brother was rubbing fenders with Richard Petty. I mean, think about it—it was huge for me. From the time I was a kid, I said, "That's what I want to do. I want to drive race cars." Those early years gave me some valuable experiences and taught me some valuable lessons that I still carry to this day. Here are a few of them:

In whatever you do, you need to have your own personal support network. My parents, brother and sisters supplied my network as a child. Now it has expanded to include my wife and children as well as my extended racing family of my crew and support staff. I have always thought that one of the cool things about racing is that it is a family endeavor. I think that is why we have such strong fan appeal. Racing, just like life, is a team sport. **If you want to be successful, you must visualize yourself as a success.** This has been an extremely important discipline for me. I believe that you need to see yourself as a winner. See yourself taking the checkered flag. This sort of vision can be applied to all aspects of life.

Dream with your eyes open. I do not remember who said it, but there is an old saying that goes something like this: "You shouldn't only dream when you are sleeping or when your eyes are closed, but you should dream with your eyes open, envisioning the possibilities." I think that I have learned to do this from a very young age. It comes from the belief that you can accomplish anything you set your mind to and that the greatest obstacles we face are the ones of our own making.

Rely on faith. I find that it takes a great deal of pressure off of me when I remember to leave life in God's hands. This philosophy comes from my conviction that there is more to who you are than what you are while you're on this Earth. I think we all get too caught up with this life. I guess it's the fear of the unknown, but not for me. I know exactly where I want my next destination to be.

Use your life accomplishments as inspiration. A couple of years ago, I ran in three marathons, the most significant being the Boston Marathon. I thought that if I could run on my feet for four and a half hours, then when I am racing it wouldn't matter how hot or how steamy it was in the South on a summer day. I could sit there for four hours on my butt for sure. I knew that this accomplishment would make me mentally stronger than my competition. So while you may look at running a marathon as an individual sport, I was doing it not only for myself, but for my team.

Be unyielding in pursuit of your dreams. Persistence and determination are powerful forces in the face of criticism. Believe me, I know. When I won the Daytona 500, I ended a 462-race winless streak. The easiest thing to do would have been to simply throw in the towel and concede to the critics, but because of my own personal conviction of my abilities, I was able to block the negative comments from adversely affecting me and actually use them as motivation.

Train yourself to think in constructive and effective ways. I believe that if you are going to be successful at any endeavor, then you need to construct a plan of what you want to do. Mark your path to success with timeline mile markers and take efficient steps to consistently achieve your goals.

Learn to use life words. *Life words* are words that build up, encourage and accentuate the positive. They are meant to counteract the destructive, negative and confidence-shattering messages that we are constantly bombarded with during tough times. The need for life words is something I am acutely aware of as I have had my share of ups and downs in my racing career. We all need to have a way to reinforce our beliefs and our commitment to our goals in the face of a world that can eventually wear you down if you let it. Use life words when you speak with others, but more importantly, use life words when you talk to yourself. Stray from sarcasm, which is very destructive.

Seek out others who share your vision for success. I was blessed to have known my friend Dale Earnhardt. Just before my win at the Daytona 500, Dale gave me a great car to drive, and he gave me unyielding confidence when he showed his faith and belief in me as a driver and told me, "You'll win in my car."

I do not know if this list is the secret to success, but so far it has worked for me. I wish you the best in your pursuit.

Michael Waltrip

Jeff Gordon's Training Wheels

Forget about style; worry about results.

Bobby Orr

Jeff's first bicycle was terrible. I'm almost embarrassed to tell you about it ... eight-inch wheels with hard rubber tires—not cool at all! All the kids were older, and he was just dying to ride his bike with all of them. There was a BMX track at the top of the street, controlled by the Police Athletic League. Jeff had training wheels on his bike. I took them off and told Jeff, "I've got to go to the office. I'll be back in a couple of hours. You need to learn to ride this bike, or I'm going to have to put it in the back of the truck and take it to the dump because I'm embarrassed to have it around the house. If you're not going to ride it, we'll get rid of it." (His mother and I, his stepfather, had this all planned out.)

We lived on a street with a little hill. I had tried to help Jeff a little bit with learning to ride, but he wasn't quite there yet. He was panic-stricken as I was leaving because he was going to lose his bike, and all the other kids had a bike, and he wouldn't have one. His mom told him, "Just learn to ride the bike. You've got two hours." After about an hour, I called home to ask how he was doing. His mom told me he was doing terrible. I said, "Okay, I'll stay out a little longer." After about two hours, I called again, and his mom told me she thought it was time for me to come on home.

I came around the corner toward the house and, sure enough, there was Jeff. He pushed off the curb and, because he was going so fast down the hill, I don't think he could fall off. He was actually pedaling his bike and riding. That's how he got started with riding.

He was so small that we had to make him a bike from scratch for his fifth birthday. I took a frame and modified it. We used wheelchair spokes because they were the lightest spokes I could find. We made magnesium forks and modified ten-speed aluminum cranks. We had the coolest bike on the block; the only one of its kind. The only thing left to do was go race it. After his mom saw a few kids much bigger than Jeff crash on bicycles, she said, "We need to find a new sport." I brought home two quarter-midget racecars.

There were tests along the way and times where we were short on money. We found ourselves in the sleeper of our pickup truck on occasion. We reduced our racing in 1987 because of money problems, but I promised myself that I would never quit. I was a quitter in school and I didn't see things through, but I was never going to quit this kid. I kept telling myself, *If I don't quit him, if I don't let him down, if I stay with this program, I think we're going to have us a race-car driver.* Who could have known that we were raising a four-time NASCAR Winston Cup champion?

John Bickford and Claire B. Lang

Angel on Your Shoulder

I love the man that can smile in trouble, that can gather strength from distress and grow brave by reflection. 'Tis the business of little minds to shrink, but he whose heart is firm and whose conscience approves his conduct will pursue his principles unto death.

Thomas Paine

My story begins in May 2001 when my mom was diagnosed with stage IV lung cancer. The cancer had been discovered at one of Mom's yearly physicals. It's amazing how something as routine as a yearly physical can be anything but that. One day everything was fine, and then the next, our world had been turned inside out forever. At first I couldn't believe she was sick. It seemed as if nothing had changed, yet with each doctor visit, the news seemed to get worse, until finally there was nothing left but to accept what was happening.

One evening at Mom's, we were sitting around and started talking—the kind of talk where you are ready to face your mortality, but still so afraid to do so. "Mom, what is the one thing that you have always wanted to do?" I asked her. "Now is the time to do it." Without hesitation, she said, "I want to go to a NASCAR race."

As long as I can remember, my mom had been one of the most die-hard NASCAR fans I had ever known. My husband Jim and I had been to a few races over the years, but Mom had never made it to one. It became my mission to find a way to get Mom to a NASCAR race. The problem was I had no idea where to start. There were so many obstacles and so little time.

I began my search on the Dale Jarrett Web site. Dale was Mom's absolute favorite driver. In fact, he was the only driver as far as she was concerned! It was a favorite family joke to get Mom going on someone who was a fan of another driver, especially a Jeff Gordon fan such as her brother Glenn. In Mom's house there'd be no cheering for anyone but Dale.

I went to the Web site and sent a letter to the "Question and Answer" page, explaining my situation, my quest to get Mom to a race and asking for any help they could provide. I also clicked on a link to Race Fans for a Cure, which while dedicated to breast cancer, I thought might be able to help. As I saw it, cancer was cancer, and any form of it was devastating.

To my delight, within five days of sending those e-mails, I received an envelope in the mail addressed to Mom from Dale Jarrett's office. I called Mom over, and the look on her face, the tears she cried as she opened an autographed picture of Dale Jarrett, were more than I could take. Dale, her absolute favorite driver, had sent her an autographed picture wishing her well and a letter to let her know he would pray for her. It instantly became her most prized possession and one she loved to show off. From that moment on, there was a connection between Dale Jarrett and my mother. He had become her friend, to help her through this awful time.

Then just two days later, I received an e-mail from Jennifer Riley with Race Fans for a Cure. She thought she could get me some tickets, but needed to know which race we wanted to go to. We were in mid-June now, and Mom was in the middle of chemo treatments. Her health deteriorated with each treatment, almost to the point where we wondered if it was worth it or not. Considering Mom's chemo treatments and the NASCAR schedule, it seemed the Brickyard 400 in August was going to be the race for Mom. We lived forty-five miles east of Indianapolis, so this was our chance!

As luck would have it, Jennifer was able to get us four tickets to the Brickyard 400 from Ford Credit, one of Dale Jarrett's sponsors. When they finally arrived, I took them to my mom.

With a look of true astonishment, she asked, "Did Dale send me these tickets?"

"Yes, Mom," I told her, "Dale sent you these tickets. He wants you to go to the race."

If she believed Dale sent her those tickets, as far as I was concerned, he did. Her excitement grew as the race got closer. She would tell anyone who hadn't heard the story before how Dale Jarrett was sending her to the race! In fact, when her sister later offered her suite passes to shield her from the sun and heat, she politely responded, "No, thank you. Dale sent me these tickets, and I don't want him thinking I'm not grateful if I'm not in that seat!"

As the chemo treatments continued, their effects on my mom got worse. But as the day of the race approached, Mom's excitement continued to build. If she wasn't feeling her best, she definitely wasn't about to let it show. Meanwhile, I began worrying about the details. *How would Mom hold up in race traffic? Where would we park so she didn't have to walk far?* Thankfully, with a few phone calls made on my lunch hour during the weeks before the race, we got it all worked out.

Finally, the day of the race arrived. Mom was feeling good. She'd had a few weeks with no chemo, so her energy level was as high as it could be. When we got to our seats after a wonderful escort to the track from the sheriff's department and a golf-cart ride to our seats from the Indianapolis Motor Speedway Safety Crew, Mom immediately made friends with everyone around her. She would tell me later, "Those NASCAR fans are just so nice. Everyone was so nice and helpful to me."

During the race, we got a few calls on my cell phone from relatives who were at the track. "Would Mom like to trade seats to be more comfortable?" they'd ask.

"No, thank you. I'm fine," she'd say. "Got to go. Dale's in the lead!"

Their questions were valid, though, as it was one of the hottest August days I could remember. It was hard on me sitting in the heat, so I could only imagine how Mom was feeling. But she never complained or regretted her decision to go to the race.

After the race, Mom was drained. You could see it in her face. Thanks to the IMS Safety Crew, getting Mom back to the car in the midst of the crowd wasn't a problem. Before we knew it, a golf cart arrived to take Mom and Dad to their car, and we were on the road in no time!

On the way home, Mom was tired, but she was happy! "If only Dale had won the race," she said, "would it have been any better!" She truly had the time of her life! And knowing that I gave her the one thing she wanted to do most before her life ended made me feel so proud.

My mother was a fighter, and she did her best to beat the cancer that had taken root in her body. On December 13, 2001, just four short months after our day at the race, Mom lost her battle with cancer. With broken hearts, we began to plan her funeral.

There was no question that we would have her Dale

Jarrett display at the funeral home. It was a big part of her, and we wanted everyone to know of her love for Dale Jarrett and NASCAR. As we spoke with our minister before the funeral, Dad told the story of how we took Mom to the race. Dad explained to him that in forty-two years of marriage, that day at the race was the most fun they had had together.

My pride and grief were overwhelming to me. During the funeral, Reverend Ballard told the story once again of my mom going to the race, calling this the best time she had had in her life. Afterward, friends and family members came up to me and told me what a wonderful thing I did for my mom. But the joy was really mine—knowing that I helped her do the one thing that was most important to her.

After the funeral, I sent a note to Kelley at Dale Jarrett's office letting her know that Mom had passed on. I received a nice condolence letter from her and Dale, telling me that Mom was now a guardian angel for him, and I truly believe that!

Dale, that little angel on your shoulder is my mom. We took care of her while she was here, and now she's taking care of you.

Lisa Hancock

My Road to the
NASCAR® Winston Cup Championship

The 2002 NASCAR Winston Cup champion.

Yeah, it feels good. Better than good, it feels great.

If I had to retype my résumé tomorrow, I would put the NASCAR Winston Cup championship at number one on the list. Including this one, I have won nine driving titles in my career, but this one is definitely my greatest accomplishment. The caliber of teams, car owners, crew chiefs and drivers in NASCAR Winston Cup alone makes everyone respect this championship. It does not take away from any of the other ones I have earned, but this one is so pressure-packed that it is an obstacle in and of itself. That is something I never had with the other championships. This NASCAR Winston Cup deal is quite a bit different. You do a lot more work here, but that is what makes it special.

When I sat down during the off-season to write this, I got to thinking about where to start. I know that a lot of people will tell you that my road to this year's championship had its fair share of bumps, but I don't judge this championship as the culmination of one season's worth of effort. Rather, my road to success has been paved with the love and support of my friends and family—people who know me for who I *really* am.

I am only thirty-one years old, but for me this championship began back in 1978 when I first wheeled a go-cart back in Westport, Indiana, at seven years old. My dad, Nelson, served as my car owner and crew chief. My father is a special man, and I credit him with much of my racing success. He never let me settle for second. He didn't like it when we ran second, and he knew that I didn't like it either. If he saw that I wasn't giving 100 percent, then he was on me pretty hard about it. He pushed me to be better. He never pressured me to be the best race-car driver in the world, but he did pressure me to be the best race-car driver that I could be. He never compared me to anybody else. He expected that what I could do was what I could do. He never said that because this guy over here could do something, that I should be able to do it, too. He pushed me hard, but he was fair about it. I think that is why you see so much fire in me today, because he always wanted me to be the best that I could be, and so do I.

As I think about this last season and how our Home Depot team rebounded from a disastrous start at Daytona (along with all of the other things we went through, some admittedly of my own making)—and to have kept our focus to go out and get the most points week in and week out—I still have a tough time believing what we have accomplished. We didn't do anything magical. It was more of a matter of pure determination—a personal victory for our race team.

I now join Jeff Gordon, Bobby Labonte, Dale Jarrett, Terry Labonte, Rusty Wallace and Bill Elliott as the only active drivers to have won a NASCAR Winston Cup championship. Pretty impressive company. It is an accomplishment that I will cherish, not only for me, but also for

my father and all of the people who have been the guideposts and mile markers down my own road—a road to the
championship.

Tony Stewart

Road to Recovery

In 1956, my parents were living in my mother's hometown of South Boston, Virginia, about two miles from the raceway. Thus began my younger brother's lifelong passion for NASCAR.

Fred was about eight years old when he and my older brother Ron used to jump on their bicycles and ride to the local racetrack when they heard the sounds of roaring engines. Some of the drivers during that time were Rex White, Ned Jarrett, Joe Weatherly, Fireball Roberts and David Pearson. Fred didn't care if the cars were racing, qualifying or just practicing. He loved to watch the cars and their drivers, and when he could get close enough, he'd pepper the mechanics with questions.

One afternoon, Fred heard a motor revving at the racetrack and took off on his bike to see who was there. He found Rex White working on his car and getting it ready for Saturday night's race. White gave the eight-year-old little boy the thrill of a lifetime by driving around the track with Fred kneeling beside him in the front of the car. Fred was hooked from that day forward.

My parents moved frequently over the next several years, but that didn't stop Fred from following the races.

He sat by the radio every weekend to listen. When my parents landed in Rock Hill, South Carolina, Fred was happy to learn there was a dirt track in town. Both local and national drivers came through to race, and Fred's love for racing continued to grow. He filled scrapbooks with articles about Roberts, Lorenzen, Jarrett, Junior Johnson and Lee Petty.

In 1961, Fred saw an advertisement in the *Charlotte Observer* about a race called the Soap Box Derby. The race would be run with homemade go-carts designed and fashioned by the contestants themselves. Fred wrote the organization for more information and was deluged with diagrams and specifications of the go-carts, how to get sponsors, how to get the car inspected and how to enter the race. Armed with all the details, Fred went to my father to beg for permission to enter. Dad promised his support, but Fred had to do the work himself. Undeterred, Fred got busy and found sponsors to help pay for materials, studied the diagrams and aerodynamics, then designed and built his car. That year was a learning experience for Fred, but the next year he won a race and placed third overall for the year.

In 1968, Fred started working with James Thrift, a local who drove a modified dirt-track car and stayed with him until Thrift retired in the 1980s. In 1970, Fred graduated from York Technical School with an Associate's Degree in automotives and began to live his dream of working on cars.

He married that same year and found in his wife, Karen, a NASCAR partner. They were at the racetracks every chance they got and agreed that Dale Earnhardt, "The Intimidator," was the epitome of NASCAR. When they had a son several years later, another Earnhardt fan was born.

When he was in his early twenties, Fred had been diagnosed with juvenile diabetes and took daily injections of insulin to regulate his blood sugar. For a kid who could always eat anything and never gain weight, this was a hard road to travel, and he had trouble keeping his diabetes under control. Karen would come home from work to find him passed out on the front porch from an insulin reaction. Once he broke his foot when his sugar got low, and he fell at the kitchen table. But the ultimate insulin reaction occurred on 1995.

The summer heat had been unbearable. Fred got up early, took his insulin, grabbed breakfast and headed for work. He and a coworker were headed down the highway in their trucks, which had no air conditioning, when Fred must have realized his blood glucose was dropping. He stopped at a convenience store and picked up a pair of crackers and a soda.

He never opened them.

His coworker, following behind Fred in her own truck, noticed Fred's truck starting to weave. She tried to raise him on the radio, but he failed to respond. She continued to try, begging him to pull off the road. As Fred's blood glucose level continued to drop, his foot became heavy on the gas pedal, pushing the truck to approximately seventy miles an hour. Suddenly, his truck veered to the right and off the road, hitting a mailbox then flipping over six or seven times before landing in a dirt field and throwing Fred through the back of the truck.

I received a phone call at the hospital where I worked as a registered nurse. My blood ran cold as I heard Fred's injuries. He had broken his neck in three areas and his back in two places, his left leg was broken, and broken ribs had punctured both of his lungs. In addition, he had a frontal closed-head injury and was in a coma with a ventilator helping him breathe. He had been taken to a trauma intensive-care unit in Charlotte, North Carolina. I was urged to hurry home, as they were not sure how long he'd live.

Sometimes being a nurse is a curse, and this was one of those times. I quickly threw some clothes in a bag, including a black dress, as my husband made arrangements for the care of the children and my job. My imagination fused with my education to form a very dismal picture, but no picture in my mind could prepare me for seeing Fred in the trauma unit some six hours later.

His head was swollen to twice its normal size, and he had screws on each side with traction attached to stabilize his head and neck. There must have been six bags of IV fluids, chest tubes to keep his lungs inflated, a catheter to drain his bladder and the breathing tube down his throat, hooked to the ventilator.

For the next two months, my brother lay in that coma, and every possible complication that could happen occurred. He developed pneumonia and gangrene, threw a blood clot to his lungs and ran extremely high fevers. Yet he never stopped fighting. I stayed two weeks after the accident, but eventually had to return home to work. Every time I had a few days off, my husband took me back on that six-hour drive.

After the first two months, although Fred was still in a coma, his health began to stabilize. The tube was removed from his mouth and a tracheotomy was performed to keep him breathing with the ventilator. We still did not know how bad his brain was injured, but we began to try to wake him up.

One weekend I stood for hours over him, rubbing his chest to elicit a response. I kept threatening to put a Rusty Wallace shirt on him if he didn't wake up. The family members all laughed, but I was crying inside because I knew that if that didn't wake him up, nothing would. The doctors told us Fred was in God's hands; they had done all they could do to help him, and now time would have to be the healer.

Miraculously, several weeks later Fred began to open his eyes, and he was moved out of trauma and into a regular room. He began to breathe on his own, and he was weaned from the ventilator. He had a long, hard road ahead of him, but the healing had finally begun. God worked his healing power, and the doctors began to call my brother the miracle boy.

Eventually, the trach was removed. Fred was very confused at first and got disoriented and frightened in the hospital, but slowly his mind began to heal also. He worked his way from bed to wheelchair and eventually to a walker.

On Christmas 1995, Fred spent the day at home with all of his family. And every gift he opened that year was . . . you guessed it . . . something to do with Dale Earnhardt— blankets, flags, cross-stitches, plaques, cars, pillows, a clock. The house looked like an Earnhardt shrine! A lot of tears were shared that day, but they were tears of joy that God had spared my brother's life.

Today, Fred walks without a cane or a walker. He no longer drives or works on cars, but that doesn't stop him from following NASCAR. He still pulls for—who else— Dale Earnhardt, Jr.

I'm so glad I didn't have to put that Rusty Wallace shirt on him.

Jan Bazen

A Special Ride

*I don't feel as though I'm a step above anyone
on this team. I'm just another link in the chain.*

Jeff Gordon

The number "24" was proudly blazoned on the sides,
but this was not my normal ride. In fact, I was not even at
the wheel. I was about to be a passenger on one of the
most amazing rides of my life.

The long 2001 NASCAR season had come to its conclu-
sion, and Rick Hendrick and I decided to visit police and
fire stations in New York City. It was really an honor to be
around these guys. They were so supportive and welcom-
ing that Rick and I quickly felt very comfortable to be in
their company.

While visiting Station 24, Ladder Company 5, I was
invited to climb into Truck 24 and take a ride in an authen-
tic New York City fire truck. Little did I know at the time
that this would be a ride I would never forget.

As soon as I climbed into the back of the truck, other
firefighters started jumping in. *Wow, these guys are really
going to give me a ride,* I thought. The firefighters continued

to pile into the truck while simultaneously climbing into their gear. "Move over!" commanded one firefighter. Another turned to me and said, "Sorry, Jeff, we're on a real call. Hold on." As incredible as it could be, I happened to climb into this fire truck only seconds before a call had come in to respond to a fire.

All of a sudden we were off with full lights flashing and sirens wailing. I was petrified and elated as this unbelievable machine flew through the streets of New York City.

The firefighters were pretty quiet during the ride except for brief outbursts of technical talk. Here I was in the middle of this, having the unique opportunity to watch these amazing men in action. They had a "look" I will never forget. It was a look of intense focus and determination. These men had as much focus on that fire, maybe more, as we have on a race car. Yeah, I get into a dangerous race car for a living, but I don't do it knowing I am putting my life on the line for another.

Luckily, the fire call ended being fairly routine (or so I was told), but I now have even more respect for these brave men than I had coming into their station, because I was able to see firsthand how brave and devoted they are in protecting the lives and property of those they serve.

God bless all of them.

Jeff Gordon

Booties First

Life's battles don't always go to the stronger or faster man; but sooner or later, the man who wins is the one who thinks he can.

C. W. Longenecker

Robert Barker sits in solitude in the depths of the NASCAR Busch Series garage, a hat professing his first career win as a crew chief spun around backward on his head.

Hidden by a stray pit cart, he receives a continuous flow of congratulatory phone calls. With each passing conversation, interrupted on occasion by a steady stream of crew-member high-fives, the dimples on his cheeks get deeper and deeper as the smile on his face spreads wider and wider.

It had been a long hard road to late September 2002. And during a brief pause from the madness, his eyes are closed, bulging arms folded across his barrel chest.

He's obviously taking it all in: the smell of his beer-drenched clothes. The sweet relaxation of a dip of snuff. Adrenaline. Gallons of it.

"It's massive. It's better than I ever thought," said Barker, who is affectionately referred to as "Bootie" throughout the industry.

"You know, I didn't think it would be, but this has got to be one of the happiest times of my life. It really is." None of this is atypical. It's a common reaction to a landmark moment in an often-unrewarding occupation. But Barker's is different. Deeper. There was no triumphant leap when Scott Wimmer took the checkered flag. There was no swan dive into his crew or standing salute from atop the pit box.

Barker is paralyzed from the waist down.

But don't try discussing it with him. He wants no extra attention for it, wants no attention at all for that matter. He won't discuss how it happened, doesn't deem it the least bit important to what he's made of himself.

Sure, his situation presents certain obstacles most don't face. But it's never fazed him, never limited his ability. He wants no sympathy.

"I think it certainly makes a bigger challenge to Bootie, to do what he does," said team owner Bill Davis. "But at the same time, he's the kind of guy who gets inspired by it, to try even harder.

"Certainly, he has to use his mind rather than his brawn, and that's his strong point. He lives and breathes this deal, and wants desperately to be successful at it. He certainly has the tools and the desire to do that."

"You won't find a harder-working individual in the garage area," Wimmer added. "People can see that and really admire him for what he does and how he does it. I hope he's with me a long time, because he sure makes my job easy."

Barker directed Davis' NASCAR Busch Series troops for nearly two years, notching four victories in the final eight races of 2002. He has achieved his life's dream—

crew chief at the NASCAR Winston Cup level.

His road to the present began at Old Dominion University (Va.), where he got the racing itch while studying mechanical engineering.

While at ODU, he volunteered on classmate Ashton Lewis' Late Model team, a role that continued after graduation. Then, having scraped together enough money to chase a dream, he headed south for Charlotte.

He knocked on every door imaginable, but was continually turned away. During that time he befriended Harold Holly, now a renowned crew chief.

Holly had no openings, but called his buddy Mike Beam, who at the time was Bill Elliott's crew chief in Hickory, North Carolina. Beam gave him a trial run that lasted some two months, but it didn't produce a full-time position.

Though unable to hire Barker, Beam did scribe a sparkling recommendation. That landed Barker on Kurt Roehrig's NASCAR Craftsman Truck Series team, where he received a deep understanding of shock technology. From there, he moved on to BDR to build shocks for Ward Burton.

In 1999, he was lured over to Jeff Gordon's Rainbow Warriors. Then, near the end of the 2000 campaign, he returned to BDR to begin life as a crew chief. It hasn't been easy.

Barker and Wimmer butted heads a bit at first. Davis said Barker might have been a bit too rough on the rookie driver, expecting more out of him than he was capable of giving at the time.

"They're both absolute racers. That's what counts in this deal. They both earned each other's respect, but it wasn't always as sweet as it is right now," Davis laughed.

Not even. Earlier on in 2002, Davis was on the verge of shutting down his sponsorless NASCAR Busch Series team. Having run the team out of his pocket for two years, it was becoming quite the financial burden. They decided to hold off and run a few more races. Wimmer ran very well, spurring a few more starts.

By the end of 2002, they had the most dominant program on the circuit.

"We were almost done, man," Barker said. "We were on the precipice, looking down on the cliff, and we came back. That makes this even more sweet. Man, this is sweet."

So sweet, it left him a blubbering mess for a while.

"He was babbling after the race, he was so excited," Davis said. "I don't know what in the world he was saying, mostly thanking me for the opportunity, I think.

"We probably did take a little bit of a chance on him, because he's not a crew chief who can climb up on top of a trailer and watch the car or get up on top of the pit box and watch the car. He's got to rely on a good support staff, which he's got.

"All these guys have been with him a long time and support him real well. If there are some areas you could call a weakness, everyone works hard around it. They appreciate so much how much he's accomplished, how focused he is and how knowledgeable he is about a race car."

The team's camaraderie was quite obvious following that first victory, as the #23 crew scooped Barker up from his wheelchair and carried him to the top of Dover's elevated Victory Lane seating area.

As he peered down on the masses, he realized the magnitude of his team's rise from the doldrums to the pinnacle of the NASCAR Busch Series ranks.

"I won a lot with (Hendrick Motorsports), but it's different when you're the crew chief," he said. "This team, we started from the bottom and we've come up together, and it means so much. We were done. Now we're a winning team. It's a good story, huh?"

Not as good as the one Barker refuses to share.

"I'm pretty tired of the *20/20, 48 Hours* feel-good story," Barker said. "I'm not a feel-good story. I'm a crew chief."

Marty Smith

The Brady Turner Story

Winners do what losers don't want to do.

H. Jackson Brown Jr.

Brady Turner was watching a NASCAR Winston Cup race at Talladega, Alabama, on television in October 1999 when he heard Ray Evernham talking directly to him.

Evernham had just announced that he'd left his job as crew chief for Jeff Gordon's Chevrolet at Hendrick Motorsports to start his own race team and help lead Dodge's return to NASCAR's top series after an absence of more than two decades.

"Ray said that as a team owner he hoped he could provide the opportunity for some people to get into racing who normally wouldn't have the chance," Turner remembers. "That comment opened my ears."

Turner was about to turn thirty. He was an African-American living near Columbus, Ohio, with his wife, Aimee, and their daughter, Amaya. He'd tinkered with his car while in high school and then got a job in an auto-salvage yard. Later, he went to work at a Honda research-and-development facility in Marysville, Ohio.

"A lot of people working there were NASCAR fans," Turner says. "Every Monday morning, the race would be the main topic of discussion. I started getting interested in it." Through a friend at work, he got a chance to go see a race in person at Michigan International Speedway. "I was hooked," he said. "I watched it constantly, and the more I watched, the more I thought the guys working on those cars had the life."

He tried to land a job after hearing about a new team being formed by former pro basketball star Julius Erving and former football star Joe Washington, but that didn't pan out. When he heard Evernham talking that day on television, he knew he'd found an opening.

First, he tried to call Evernham. He tracked down a phone number for the shop where Evernham was in the very early stages of pulling his team together. When he called, Evernham was off at another race. He would be back on Monday, the secretary said.

It's only a seven-and-a-half- or eight-hour drive, Turner thought.

So he left Columbus late Sunday afternoon. He stopped at a welcome center just inside the North Carolina state line and slept a couple of hours. He woke up, splashed some water on his face, put on a clean shirt and finished the drive to Evernham's shop.

He was there at 7 A.M. So was Evernham.

"I was so impressed," Evernham says. "He took a big chance and showed he was willing to make the sacrifices and do what it takes to be a success."

Still, Evernham wasn't about to hire Turner just because he showed up. He did give Turner his phone number and a promise.

"We said we would try to get something together where I could come work for a couple of weeks," Turner said. "Early the next March, I had three weeks of vacation built up, and I took them all. I came down and worked at his shop."

He did whatever needed to be done. Evernham was still impressed. This time, when he went back to Ohio, he had more than a phone number. He had a job offer.

The Turners moved to North Carolina at the end of that summer. Turner now is a member of the team that fields the #9 Dodges for driver Bill Elliott, working at the shop through the week and flying to the track on Sunday morning on a charter flight that brings in the race-day crews for each race, then returns to Charlotte that night.

"I basically started right at the bottom," Turner said. "I was running errands to pick up parts, cleaning up the shop. I worked my way up to cleaning and fabricating parts. On race days, I've taken care of the windshield tear-offs. I run gas, pull the front air hose and catch the left-front tire."

Turner is paying his dues.

"He has done everything we've asked him to do," Evernham said. "He wants to learn everything because one day he wants to be a crew chief."

That's a lofty goal.

"I have a lot of wild and crazy ambitions to do a lot of different things," Turner admits. "I want to learn as much as I can about the sport, but I try not to get overly excited about getting a position too early or about accomplishing anything without being prepared. I want to make this a career where I learn as I go, and once I get a spot I want to be able to do it."

He's one of only a few African-Americans working full-time in NASCAR's top series. While he hopes that will change, Turner tries his best to keep that part of his story in perspective.

"Since I have been out of high school, every job I've had I was the black guy in the shop," he said. "It's something I have always dealt with, so I learned how to deal with all of the attitudes at an early age. Race doesn't seem like an issue to me."

The job took the Turners from their home in Ohio and now takes Brady away from home each weekend. Aimee and Amaya are proud of what he does and what he wants to do.

"It shows that with a lot of hard work, effort and dedication, your dreams are endless," Aimee Turner says. "He is not a person who has celebrity status or anything of that nature, but to me he is a celebrity and a role model in my heart.

"It is stories like this that should give everyday people the incentive to live life to the fullest."

David Poole

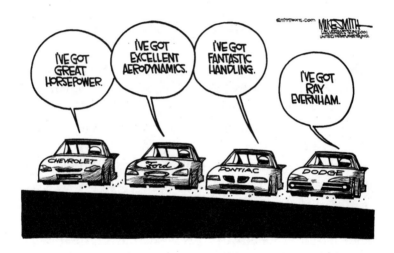

Reprinted by permission of Mike Smith, Las Vegas Sun.

The Power of Determination

I have been asked many times what I think is the most important attribute to have as a NASCAR Winston Cup driver. To me the answer is easy: *determination.*

Without the determination of an iron will, then self-doubt, critics and circumstance can end a racing career before it starts. Take, for example, the risks I took. When I think back on it, I still can't believe it.

I was just a kid working at my father's sawmill near Hickory, North Carolina, when construction started on the Hickory Motor Speedway. It was the talk of the town, and every person in little Hickory was very excited. I made a commitment to myself that I would somehow work it out, that I would be a part of that first race. Although I was only twenty years old when the track opened, I had saved a little money from working at the mill, and I invested, along with my friend John Lentz, in a 1939 Ford coupe. We agreed that I should drive, and in my first race I finished tenth.

Unfortunately, at that time my father did not share my enthusiasm, and he informed me he didn't want me racing. I respected my father's wishes, and months went by when I did not climb behind the wheel of that car, instead

letting John pilot the coupe while I worked the pits. One
night, just before the start of a race, John showed up at
the track feeling very ill. "Ned, there is no way I can drive
tonight. If we're going to be in this race, you will have to
drive," he said.

John and I looked very similar, so few noticed when I
climbed in the car in his place. That night I finished second, our team's best finish to date. Right there, John and I
decided that it would be best if I drove the car from then
on, running under the name of John Lentz in order to
avoid my father's wrath. We continued to post strong fin-
ishes until one week we ended up winning the race. Well,
I could hardly avoid the Victory Lane celebration, and in
short order word got back to my dad that I had been driving the car. To my surprise, my father did not scold me,
but rather, he said that if I was determined to do the driving, then I should at least get the credit for my work.

In 1956, I moved up to what was then the equivalent of
the NASCAR Busch Series and had a great season, finishing second to Ralph Earnhardt in the battle for the
national title. I would end up winning the title in 1957 and
1958 and yearned for more. Opportunity was not far
behind.

I was determined to make it to the big time and race in
what today has become the NASCAR Winston Cup Series.
My timing, unfortunately, could not have been worse.
Sponsors were very rare at that time, and there simply
wasn't any money floating around the sport. I decided
that the only way I was going to make it was if I bought
my own car. I declared my intentions to my friends, who
promptly informed me I was crazy.

I heard that a '57 Ford that had been successfully driven by Junior Johnson was for sale for $2,000. Well, it may
as well have been selling for $2,000,000, because I was
almost broke, but I did have a plan. I figured that if I wrote

the guy selling the car a check late on a Friday afternoon, he would not have time to cash it until Monday morning. That weekend there were races in Myrtle Beach, South Carolina, and Charlotte, North Carolina, on consecutive nights. Each paid $950 for first place. I figured that I could win both races for $1,900, and then I would scrounge up the balance to cover the check before the bank opened on Monday.

We would arrive at the track in Myrtle Beach too late to practice, but nonetheless, I qualified eighth. The field was brutally tough for the race, and soon we fought our way up to the front and held on for the victory. While I had just completed the first half of my plan, my enthusiasm would be cut short by a piercing reality. You see, in those days, we used to wrap the steering wheels with black electrical tape in order to build them up. Well, in the haste of the transaction and our sprint over to Myrtle Beach, none of us noticed that whoever wrapped the steering wheel on the car had wound it backwards, causing the edges to dig into my hands like razor blades. By the end of the race, the tape had literally chewed the meat off my hands. We had to wrap a tourniquet around my arm to stop the bleeding for the Victory Lane celebration.

The ride to Charlotte was three and a half hours long, and along the way I had to stop at the hospital to get my wounds bandaged. We arrived in Charlotte in the middle of the night and immediately started working on the car. I started the race, but soon realized that due to the severity of the injuries to my hands, there was no way I could finish it. Finally, I simply could take no more of it, and I brought the car in to the pits. By a stroke of luck, Junior Johnson stood nearby as his car had been put out of the race a little earlier. Junior agreed to jump in to replace me as the driver, and because this was a car he was already very familiar with, he guided it to victory. Having started the race, I got credit for the victory. Word had already spread throughout the pits about my needing to win both races in order to cover the purchase price for the race car, so Junior refused to take any part of the winnings, and I had accomplished what I set out to do.

I would go on to win forty-eight more times, including two championships in 1961 and 1965.

So you see, *determination* is a powerful force. Even when your better judgment suggests otherwise, I firmly believe that if you want something bad enough and are willing to work very hard to make it happen, you can accomplish great things.

Ned Jarrett

[EDITORS' NOTE: *Ned Jarrett ran that 1957 Ford in five races, winning three times and finishing second and third once.*]

Reprinted by permission of Matt Dorton/TRACK LAUGHS.

Brothers at Their Best

Our family is modest, so we don't talk about things like this much, but I'll never forget that day in Atlanta. When it was over, Terry and I just said, "Man, I just can't believe that happened." It was a great day for all of our family—our wives, our mom and dad were all there.

My brother, Terry, and I were not close friends while I was growing up. There were eight years between us, so we had different friends. Both of us were born in Corpus Christi, Texas. Terry grew up mostly in Texas and was off racing all over the state. My growing-up years were more in North Carolina, having moved there with my family when I was still in school. Now that Terry and I live near each other and are racing in the same series, we have gotten much closer and are good friends.

It just happened in November 1996 that we went to Atlanta for the last race of the year. We couldn't have planned it any better if we'd wanted to. Terry was leading in points for the NASCAR Winston Cup championship, and it had been about twelve years since his last and only championship, so I knew that it would mean so much to him to win this championship. Terry needed a good finish to win. If Jeff Gordon (second in points) won the race,

Terry would have to finish eighth or ninth. Terry was looking for his second championship. I was looking for my first win of the season. I had won three races in the last year, but none this year. So both of us were on a mission.

We went out to qualify: I won the pole, and Terry started third. Jeff Gordon was second. Terry had struggled with a broken hand since the last race at Phoenix. He didn't get to practice much and wasn't feeling well. The night before the race, Terry said to me, "Man, I sure do need to lead a lap tomorrow." I assured him that I would do all that I could to help him do that. We also did something very unusual for us to do before a race: We talked about how neat it would be for me to win the race and him to win the championship.

The next morning as I was walking to my car, the Atlanta track public-relations guy told me to be sure to come to Victory Lane if Terry won the championship. I commented that I was hoping to be there already. I could not believe that I was saying this, but I did feel good about the race.

I jumped out front at the green flag and led the race. Jeff had some tire problems and had to pit. Terry drove up to me, and I let him pass me so that he could collect five bonus points for leading a lap. We both ran well all day. All during the race, I kept up with Terry's position on the track. Never for a moment did I lose sight of where he was and where he needed to be to win the championship. Near the end of the race, Terry dropped back after a pit stop. I knew that he needed to finish in the top five or better to be safe, but Gordon had worked his way back to the front and was still running well, too. I was focused on what I had to do, but it was kind of neat to know what was going on with Terry. The checkered flag waved in the air as I crossed the finish line first. I had won my first race of the season. Gordon finished third. Terry won the championship with a fifth-place finish.

Then it happened! Terry and I hadn't discussed anything about what we would do in this situation. After a win, I usually head down pit road to Victory Circle. I just never do unusual things like victory laps or cutting doughnuts on the front stretch. As I was about to turn off the racetrack onto pit road, I noticed Terry drive by on the way to meet the Winston people (series sponsors) on the backstretch, who then would escort him to the front stretch for his celebration. At the last second, I swerved back onto the track to join Terry. We suddenly found ourselves side by side riding around the track together. (That made lots of headlines.) It was awfully exciting! I looked over at Terry and gave him a "thumbs-up." The fans were going crazy, screaming at us with excitement. My thoughts turned to the uniqueness of this event—one that is so rare in racing that it had never happened before in NASCAR and probably will not happen again for many years to come.

As I drove alongside Terry, I started thinking about what we had talked about the night before. I just couldn't believe we had said something that actually became reality. My excitement was more for my parents. How neat it was for them. I pictured them walking proudly to the victory celebrations for their two sons. I thought of my mom and dad having two children, and both of them winning today in the same race. That is something I'll cherish forever. I won the race, and Terry won the championship.

Bobby Labonte with Max Helton

Go to a Race

I had an interesting discussion with a guy I work with named Bob. It went something like this:

Bob: "Hey, Rob, I hear you are going to Homestead for the race this weekend."

Rob: "Yup, we are leaving Saturday morning. I can't wait!"

Bob: "I don't understand what you people see in that. I have tried watching it a few times, and they just drive around in circles. It's boring. Unless, of course, they crash."

Ever had this conversation? I can't tell you how many times I have heard the same old lines. Okay, I agree, at times, to the untrained eye, racing can appear to be guys going in circles, but if you really pay attention, there is so much more.

Back to my point. My buddies kept asking me what the running order was. I knew what position each driver was in through the lead lap and even back through the guys a lap down. I get so involved that I follow every move, every pit stop, every slip and slide. At any given time if the scoring computers went down, I could have reset the field from memory, and I didn't even have a scanner on. From home you get to see one part of the race at any given time.

In between ninety-plus commercials per race, they try to show you a battle here or there for position and any contact that may be made. There is always something going on at all times at any point during the race. If you have never been to a race, GO!!! And if you can, spend a few extra bucks and buy or rent a scanner. The things you will hear the crews talking about are priceless, and it really adds to each driver's persona. Whenever someone tells me that racing is boring, I ask, "How many races have you been to?" and the answer is always "None." You can not appreciate the full intensity of the sport from behind the television. Drama is being there, smelling the racing fuel and tire smoke, and watching these cars go by in a blur. They aren't driving in circles. They are driving full speed in a straight line toward a concrete wall as fast as they can. They are playing a game of chicken with the wall knowing it won't move. At the last possible moment, they turn the wheel and, at some tracks, slam the brakes. They slide through the corners on the verge of spinning out and, just as they catch their breath, they mash the gas and do it all over again. This is good stuff.

When we were younger, my friends and I would cruise across parking lots at fifty miles per hour, cut the wheel and jack the brakes, and spin the car out. It was fun. These guys are doing it at 180 miles per hour, and somehow they don't spin out.

There is so much more involved during the race. There is pit strategy, the choreographed dance called "4 tires and fuel in 13.5," and there is always a little rubbing and banging. Race weekend involves so many things. There are displays from the sponsors with activities and games. Think you can change tires as fast as the big boys? Try your luck at the Home Depot trailer with their pit-stop challenge. Rubbermaid had a display one weekend where they gave you a baseball bat and challenged you to break their products. Pfizer had free health screenings. Pontiac was giving away a Limited Edition Pace Car. Drivers were signing autographs, and there were more free items up for grabs. The souvenir trucks were in full bloom, allowing you to sport your favorite driver's colors as a hat, shirt, license plate, sticker, inflatable car, flag, blanket, underwear, anything and everything!

So tell your boss you are taking a half-day one Friday afternoon. Tell him you have a doctor's appointment; tell him you have to pick up relatives at the airport; tell him your dog has the flu. Do whatever it takes and get to a race. Do not tell me how boring it is until you go. And if you spend a race weekend at the track and your heart doesn't pound when they fire the engines, and if your breath isn't taken as they battle three wide into the turns, then go to the Pfizer tent and get a check-up.

I probably didn't do a great job explaining the rush I get at the track and how that carries over to watching it on television. But that is my point. It is a feeling that can't be explained. It needs to be experienced. Are you experienced? Go to a race!!!!!!

Rob Faiella

Reprinted by permission of Mike Smith, Las Vegas Sun.

Creating a Dynasty of Values

When I was born, Mother and Daddy lived with my grandmother and granddaddy. There were three brothers and four sisters all living in the same rural house with no running water or electricity. We had twelve or fourteen people living beside the shop. We were poor, but we didn't know it because all the neighbors were the same way.

My little brother, Maurice, and I were always getting into scrapes with each other. I've got scars all over my head, and he has scars all over his. Our social lives were completely different, but when we were at home we played together and worked together.

I played football and basketball in high school. Most of the guys who played ball stayed after school for practice and games, then went home to plow a field or milk a cow or something. I'd go home and work on a race car.

My dad was pretty stern with us, but he could be very compassionate. In business dealings, he didn't have contracts. He gave his word and made sure he got it done; it didn't make a difference how much of a hardship it was on him. He taught us that you are responsible for what you say and for what you do.

Mother was a peacemaker. She tried to keep the home fires burning while Dad was out racing or doing other

things, and she got us off to church every Sunday morning.
Daddy was always a mechanic. He had a bunch of
trucks and hauled anything for anybody. He did a little
truck farming, too, with a few things he raised. In 1949,
when the NASCAR Winston Cup Series first started, he
got his first race car—a '37 Plymouth with a straight 8
Buick motor in it. People came from Daytona, Atlanta and
all around to race. It was big money even back then. Dad
read in the paper that Bill France was having a race in
Charlotte. Dad hung out at a service station on the south
side of Greensboro with some of his buddies. One of them
had a '47 or '48 Buick. It ran really fast on the road. Dad
and his brother talked the guy into borrowing the thing
so we could race it in Charlotte.

We drove that car over to Charlotte and pulled into a
Texaco station, put it on a lift, changed the oil, greased it
and got ready to race. That's all there was at the time to
make a race car. Dad got about halfway through the race
when the sway bar broke. The thing turned over with
them, tearing off all four doors. We had to thumb a ride
back with my uncle to get home. Even after all that, my
dad said, "You know, I think I might like this racin'." He
went out and bought the smallest car he could, which was
a 1949 Plymouth Coupe. It didn't even have a back seat. I
think it went for $890 and they could win $1,500, so it was
a great deal.

I don't think that Mother thought a lot about what
Daddy did when he sold his truck and trucking business
and stopped farming the land. He said, "Okay, we're goin'
in the racin' business." This was a new venture, and he
didn't know if it was going to work. The first year they
only ran about eight races, but he had made the commitment. He was probably the first one to say, "I can make a
living out of this if I watch what I do." It was a family business from the beginning. We didn't have help, and Daddy
did all the work. As long as we got enough money racing

on Sunday to get back to the race the next week, he was happy. When we first started racing, he was not that fast. He figured out that there were 200 laps, and he wanted to make it to the end of the 200 laps. If he led for 195 laps and then fell out, he wouldn't make it back to race the next week. They called him "Mr. Consistency." He might not win first, but he wound up winning more races than anybody at that time. He was always second, third or fourth. He won enough money to get us something to eat so that we could go to the next race.

I started working on the cars when I was about eleven years old. I wasn't really interested in driving them. I graduated high school and went to King's Business College in Greensboro. I took an eight-month business course, but it took me two years to get though it. I went four months during winter, and then when the '57 season started I came back and started working on the race car. Even when I went to school, I'd go during the day and work on the car at night. When we had to start going to the races, I couldn't go to school at all.

When I turned eighteen, I went in one day and said, "Okay, Dad, I want to drive a race car." He said, "You're too young." I told him, "Buddy Baker's driving." But he said it didn't make a difference. He told me I couldn't race until I was twenty-one. "You'll do a lot of growing up between the years of eighteen and twenty-one," he said, and he was right. I got out into the world and experienced a lot more during those years.

I walked in one day and said, "Okay, I'm twenty-one." He said, "There's a car over in the corner. Get it ready." It was a convertible. Dale Inman, Red Myler and I loaded it up and headed for Columbia, South Carolina. I had never been in a race in my life, but they threw me right out there and away I went. It took me a long time to learn to drive, but we finally brought in a winner.

I met Linda early in my racing career. We dated a couple

of years, but I was out of town a lot. One night I told her, "You know I love you, and if we are ever thinking about getting married, we need to do it now because I'm not going to have time later." She said, "Okay." We went to South Carolina and got married one night. When we came home she didn't tell anybody besides her parents that we were married; not even my parents knew. It took about three months for me to get up the money to buy her a ring. After I gave her the ring, she told everybody.

A little over a year later, we were living with Mother and Daddy when Kyle was born in the same house that I was born in. Linda and I saved up some money and bought a mobile home and put it in their front yard. Within twelve months, our daughter, Sharon, came along, and that place seemed to get even smaller. We didn't have air conditioning in the trailer, but we had a '60s Chrysler with air conditioning. We'd eat supper, put the kids in the car, and go out and ride around until they went to sleep. Then we'd come home and put them in bed.

When I was home, we did things together, like playing ball or taking them to the movies. When I was on the road, Linda took care of things. In the summertime, we took the family with us everywhere. I had one of the children in each hand, and Linda would have the third one along with the diaper bags. We put the little ones in the back seat, and we went because that was our family. We just did it the way my mother and daddy did it.

I was fortunate to be with NASCAR Winston Cup racing as it was growing. We were driving an offbeat car—a Plymouth. We won twenty-seven races in one year, and people screamed for us to win more. Right at the time that my career was taking off, Dad's was winding down. He won the championship in '58 and '59. He was third or fourth in the points standing in '60, and then I think he won only one race in '61; then he got hurt at Daytona, and that was basically the end of his career. He and Johnny

Beauchamp got together right at the end of a 100-mile race, and they went through the fence and turned the car over, demolishing everything. They carried him off to the hospital with a punctured lung, a torn-up knee and a broken leg. A bunch of people came in to donate blood. For two or three days he laid there, and they just tried to keep him alive. I went in, and he said, "Come here." I leaned over. "You and Maurice go on home and go up to Greensboro and buy another car. Mother and me will be home about Friday." He was home on Friday—about four months later. That's how badly he was hurt, but he was ready to go. "Let's go racin' again."

I've had some bad wrecks and been beaten up pretty badly, but if I can wake up and see the ceiling, I know that it's okay. After some of the wrecks, I could remember everything that happened, and with others, I could only remember part of it. I think that the good Lord has got a little mechanism in us that, when you get close to death, causes you not to remember. It seems like he blocks that out of your memory so that you don't wake up in the middle of the night screaming with the terror of it. The big wreck at Daytona in '88 was spectacular. But I felt like a guardian angel said, "This is going to be a bad wreck," then took me out of the car, turned it over and then stuck me back in. I know this has happened more than once because I've seen some of the wrecks and I say, "No way are you going to get out of there without getting hurt." I'm usually conscious of what's going on, and most of the time I can get out of the car by myself. At Daytona I remember the doctor coming to the side of the car and asking, "Are you okay?" I said, "Yeah, I'm okay. I just can't see anything." I was blinded for probably five minutes, but the doctor said my sight would come back, and it did. It wasn't until after I had seen the films of the accident that I knew that the car had turned over.

Linda came to the hospital, and I could tell she had

been crying. Once she knew everything was fine, though, she was mad. She had gotten over the hurt part and moved on to anger. All the times we talked about racing and accidents that happened, we had reached an agreement. I always told her, "When we are not having fun anymore, I'm not going to do this." She came in there gritting her teeth and said, "Are we having fun?" Everybody just broke up laughing, and any hurting I had just went away.

It hurts a lot more to see someone you love hurt than to be hurt yourself. When Kyle was hurt in Talledaga, Linda and I went in to see him. I felt like we were hurting even worse than he was, and we couldn't help but wonder who was to blame.

After Kyle's son Adam was killed in the accident, we got hundreds and hundreds of letters from fans. One lady wrote, "Never put a question mark where God has put a period." I settled right down after I heard that. I said, "Okay, I'm not going to question anymore." We have to go forward with our lives.

One thing I've never questioned is who's responsible for my making it in this business. The racetracks have never paid Richard Petty a penny; the sponsors have never paid me anything. If it weren't for the fans, I wouldn't be out there in the first place. After my first race I signed one autograph; my second race I signed two. I have always looked at the fans as the guys who were paying the bills. Every time I sign an autograph, it's like saying, "Thank you for letting me do what I want to do and make a living out of it."

I thank God for my family.
I thank God for my fans.

Richard Petty

More Chicken Soup?

Many of the stories and poems you have read in this book were submitted by readers like you who had read earlier *Chicken Soup for the Soul* books. We publish at least five or six *Chicken Soup for the Soul* books every year. We invite you to contribute a story to one of these future volumes.

Stories may be up to 1,200 words and must uplift or inspire. You may submit an original piece, something you have read or your favorite quotation on your refrigerator door.

To obtain a copy of our submission guidelines and a listing of upcoming *Chicken Soup* books, please write, fax or check our Web sites.

Please send your submissions to:

Chicken Soup for the Soul
P.O. Box 30880, Santa Barbara, CA 93130
fax: 805-563-2945
Web site: *www.chickensoupforthesoul.com*

Just send a copy of your stories and other pieces to the above address.

We will be sure that both you and the author are credited for your submission.

For information about speaking engagements, other books, audiotapes, workshops and training programs, please contact any of our authors directly.

Supporting Others

VICTORY JUNCTION GANG.

Founded for kids by Kyle and Pattie Petty
in honor of Adam Petty

The Victory Junction Gang Camp, founded by Kyle and Pattie Petty in honor of their son Adam, will bring the energy, excitement and traditions of auto racing to the medical camping experience. When the first campers come through the "Winner's Archway" and enter the camp in summer 2004, Victory Junction will be a magical, memorable and medically advanced place where children living with life-threatening and chronic illnesses—and their families—will be changed by fueling them with memories of fun, friendship, achievement, success and empowerment.

When complete, Victory Junction's seventy-five-acre site will have more than thirty-six buildings, including a dining hall, gym, pool, theater, therapeutic equestrian center, arts and crafts center, race shop and sixteen cabins. Most importantly, the camp will offer a sophisticated medical facility staffed by a team of professionals capable of administering to the needs of these children, up to and including the administering of chemotherapy.

Children ages seven to fifteen will attend Victory Junction at no cost to their families. Victory Junction is located in the Piedmont Triad area of North Carolina and will be open year round. At Victory Junction, camp's not over until every child experiences the thrill of Victory Lane!

The Victory Junction Gang Camp
311 Branson Mill Road
Randleman, NC 27317
336-498-9055
www.victoryjunction.org

The goal of **Motor Racing Outreach** (**MRO**) is to introduce the racing community (racers and fans) to a personal faith in Christ, growth in Christlikeness and active involvement in a local church through relationships that provide care, sharing knowledge of God's word and assistance in developing their leadership skills. MRO is a nonprofit 501(c)(3) organization founded in 1988 when founder Max Helton was summoned by three drivers on the NASCAR Winston Cup circuit to minister in their unusual situation, as racers and their families are rarely able to attend "normal" church services.

As MRO developed, a similar need was apparent in motorsports across the board, from automobiles to motorcycles to powerboats.

Motor Racing Outreach
Smith Tower, Suite 405
5555 Concord Parkway South
Concord, NC 28027
phone: 704-455-3828
fax: 704-455-5806
e-mail: *info@go2mro.com*

Who Is Jack Canfield?

Jack Canfield is one of America's leading experts in the development of human potential and personal effectiveness. He is both a dynamic, entertaining speaker and a highly sought-after trainer. Jack has a wonderful ability to inform and inspire audiences toward increased levels of self-esteem and peak performance.

He is the author and narrator of several bestselling audio- and videocassette programs, including *Self-Esteem and Peak Performance, How to Build High Self-Esteem, Self-Esteem in the Classroom* and *Chicken Soup for the Soul—Live*. He is regularly seen on television shows such as *Good Morning America, 20/20* and *NBC Nightly News*. Jack has co-authored numerous books, including the *Chicken Soup for the Soul* series, *Dare to Win* and *The Aladdin Factor* (all with Mark Victor Hansen), *100 Ways to Build Self-Concept in the Classroom* (with Harold C. Wells), *Heart at Work* (with Jacqueline Miller) and *The Power of Focus* (with Les Hewitt and Mark Victor Hansen).

Jack is a regularly featured speaker for professional associations, school districts, government agencies, churches, hospitals, sales organizations and corporations. His clients have included the American Dental Association, the American Management Association, AT&T, Campbell's Soup, Clairol, Domino's Pizza, GE, ITT, Hartford Insurance, Johnson & Johnson, the Million Dollar Roundtable, NCR, New England Telephone, Re/Max, Scott Paper, TRW and Virgin Records. Jack is also on the faculty of Income Builders International, a school for entrepreneurs.

Jack conducts an annual eight-day Training of Trainers program in the areas of self-esteem and peak performance. It attracts educators, counselors, parenting trainers, corporate trainers, professional speakers, ministers and others interested in developing their speaking and seminar-leading skills.

For further information about Jack's books, tapes and training programs, or to schedule him for a presentation, please contact:

Self-Esteem Seminars
P.O. Box 30880
Santa Barbara, CA 93130
phone: 805-563-2935 • fax: 805-563-2945
Web site: *www.chickensoupforthesoul.com*

Who Is Mark Victor Hansen?

Mark Victor Hansen is a professional speaker who, in the last twenty years, has made over four thousand presentations to more than 2 million people in thirty-three countries. His presentations cover sales excellence and strategies; personal empowerment and development; and how to triple your income and double your time off.

Mark has spent a lifetime dedicated to his mission of making a profound and positive difference in people's lives. Throughout his career, he has inspired hundreds of thousands of people to create a more powerful and purposeful future for themselves while stimulating the sale of billions of dollars worth of goods and services.

Mark is a prolific writer and has authored *Future Diary, How to Achieve Total Prosperity* and *The Miracle of Tithing.* He is the coauthor of the *Chicken Soup for the Soul* series, *Dare to Win* and *The Aladdin Factor* (all with Jack Canfield) and *The Master Motivator* (with Joe Batten).

Mark has also produced a complete library of personal empowerment audio- and videocassette programs that have enabled his listeners to recognize and better use their innate abilities in their business and personal lives. His message has made him a popular television and radio personality with appearances on ABC, NBC, CBS, HBO, PBS, QVC and CNN.

He has also appeared on the cover of numerous magazines, including *Success, Entrepreneur* and *Changes.*

Mark is a big man with a heart and a spirit to match—an inspiration to all who seek to better themselves.

For further information about Mark, please contact:

Mark Victor Hansen & Associates
P.O. Box 7665
Newport Beach, CA 92658
phone: 949-759-9304 or 800-433-2314
fax: 949-722-6912
Web site: *www.chickensoupforthesoul.com*

Who Is Matthew E. Adams?

Matthew E. Adams is a bestselling author, professional speaker and entrepreneur who is committed to improving the lives of others. Matthew coauthored *Chicken Soup for the Soul of America*, in addition to contributing to numerous other *Chicken Soup for the Soul* projects. Matthew is a media and marketing consultant with extensive radio and television experience. He began his career at ESPN, and can be seen regularly as a golf-industry analyst and equipment expert on The Golf Channel. Matthew travels extensively as a "Life Strategies" professional speaker concentrating on academic and corporate presentations.

Matthew worked directly with many of NASCAR's biggest stars in putting together this book, including Jeff Gordon, Bobby Labonte, Michael Waltrip, Tony Stewart, Ricky Rudd and John Andretti, among others.

"The drivers, their PR directors and the entire NASCAR community have been overwhelmingly supportive of this book. I have worked with many professional athletes and major sports organizations and have found NASCAR to be the most accommodating and friendliest people to work with. It is no surprise the sport is so successful," says Matthew.

If you wish to contact Matthew or schedule him for your next event, he can be reached by e-mail at *tempogolf123@aol.com* or at:

Adams and Company
P.O. Box 1738
North Kingstown, RI 02852
Web site: *www.chickensoupforthesoul.com*

Jeff Gordon and Matthew Adams

Who Is Jeff Aubery?

Introduced to the golf industry at an early age, Jeff was mentored personally and professionally by Nat C. Rosasco, owner of Northwestern Golf Co. Now an entrepreneur in his own right, Jeff founded and is the president of Golf Sales West, Inc./Tornado Golf, the world's largest original equipment golf-bag manufacturer.

Jeff has been committed to golf as a lifetime passion and has traveled the world extensively in pursuit of the game and the industry that surrounds it. Jeff is most proud of his tireless work to help bring millions of people to the game of golf by developing programs and products that are accessible and affordable for everyone.

Jeff is an active sponsor of junior golf programs and charity golf tournaments all over the world. Jeff makes time for a round of golf whenever possible and has enjoyed playing with some of the greatest names in the sport at many of the world's most famous courses.

Jeff is a two-time *New York Times* #1 bestselling author in addition to a *USA Today* and *Publishers Weekly* bestselling author. Jeff's books have sold millions of copies worldwide, and he is a veteran of hundreds of radio and television interviews.

Coauthor of *Chicken Soup for the Golfer's Soul, Chicken Soup for the Father's Soul* and *Chicken Soup for the Golfer's Soul: The Second Round,* Jeff is no stranger to the *Chicken Soup* phenomenon. Jeff is married to Patty Aubery, coauthor of *Chicken Soup for the Christian Soul, Chicken Soup for the Christian Family Soul, Chicken Soup for the Christian Teenage Soul, Chicken Soup for the Surviving Soul* and *Chicken Soup for the Expectant Mother's Soul.*

The couple and their two sons, Jeffrey Terrance and Chandler Scott, make their home in Santa Barbara, California. Jeff is a dynamic and enthusiastic speaker and is available for personal appearances. He can be reached at:

Golf Sales West, Inc./Tornado Golf
2100 Eastman Ave., Suite A
Oxnard, CA 93030
phone: 800-GOLF-BAG
e-mail: *SoupStory@aol.com*

Who Is Kirk Autio?

Kirk H. Autio has an extensive background in the field of large, high-end commercial construction projects and currently serves as private consultant to a select group of national and regional contracting firms. His specialty fields in addition to commercial construction include land use and development, natural-disaster cleanup and various specialty trades.

To date, Kirk has been instrumental in the startup of numerous companies, large and small, throughout the southwestern United States. Kirk has recently teamed up with longtime friend Mike Hadden, assisting him with the creation and development of intellectual property relating to ball cap visor technology, which is utilized in many sporting arenas such as NASCAR, NFL, MLB and the PGA. Kirk attributes much of his business success to date to his close friend and mentor Robert D. Knudtson of Panatoni Development, Mike Moore of Southland Industries, Inc., and the strong, loving support of his wife Nancy.

Kirk has been coined a "motor head" for many years, dating back to his high-school days where he often could be found under the hood wrenching on his small-block Chevys and then putting them to the test. He has been an avid NASCAR fan for almost two decades and cheers for the green #18. He lives with his wife Nancy and daughter Molly in Santa Barbara, California. NASCAR aside, his hobbies include hunting, fishing, golfing and surfing in front of his beachfront home in Mexico.

Kirk is a dynamic speaker who is associated with Toastmasters International as well as the National Speakers Association and is available for speaking engagements. Kirk may be contacted at:

P.O. Box 30880
Santa Barbara, CA 93101
phone: 805-898-0070
e-mail: *kautio@chickensoupforthesoul.com*
Web site: *www.kirkautio.com*

Contributors

Several of the stories in this book were taken from previously published sources, such as books, magazines and newspapers. These sources are acknowledged in the permissions section. If you would like to contact any of the contributors for information about their writing or would like to invite them to speak in your community, look for their contact information included in their biography. The remainder of the stories were submitted by readers of our previous *Chicken Soup for the Soul* books who responded to our requests for stories. We have also included information about them.

Liz Allison was married to NASCAR Winston Cup driver, Davey Allison, until his untimely death in July 1993. Liz has written three books. Her newest title, *NASCAR Wives: The Women Behind the Sunday Drivers,* became available in May 2002 (*www.umipub.com*). Liz has worked as a race-day reporter for TNT Sports and has written articles for various publications. She resides in Nashville with her two children, Robbie and Krista, and her husband, Ryan Hackett. To have Liz Allison speak at your event, contact The Nashville Speakers Bureau at 615-263-4143. Liz also welcomes your e-mails at *alli65@aol.com.*

Janice Bazen worked as an R.N. until 2000. After taking an early retirement, she began writing human-interest and NASCAR stories. She enjoys reading and fishing and plans to continue her writing. Read more of Janice's work on-line at "The Car Guy of Benchfield." Contact Janice at *bazenjan@hotmail.com.*

John Bickford, Executive Vice President of Action Performance Companies, Inc., is a motorsports veteran who has been involved in racing for forty years. He is the owner of MPD Racing, a products leader in open-wheel racing components and builder of the famous Pit Boss racing jacks used by over half of the Winston Cup teams.

Steve Byrnes is a pit reporter for NASCAR on the Fox broadcast team. He also hosts *Totally NASCAR* on Fox Sports Net and *Trackside* for the Speed Channel. Byrnes has worked as broadcast journalist in NASCAR since 1985. He and his wife Karen are the proud parents of Bryson Byrnes.

Ron Camacho went NASCAR and self-published *From the Heart of Racing* after coauthoring *Chicken Soup for the Country Soul.* A contributor to *Chicken Soup for the NASCAR Soul,* Ron offers more of the same when you contact A Healing Voice Publishing at 615-372-0621. Be looking for his new releases, *The Last Dragon* and *From the Heart and the Drill: Staying Safe, Sane and Sober in a Post–911 Economy.* E-mail Ron at *roncamacho@aol.com.*

Michele Wallace Campanelli is a national bestselling author. She was born on the Space Coast of Florida where she resides with her husband, Louis V.

Campanelli III. She is the author of over twenty-two short-story books, fiction novels and e-books. Her personal editor is Fontaine M. Wallace. Michele can be e-mailed at *www.michelecampanelli.com.*

Sherryl Creekmore is a full-time freelance photojournalist on the NASCAR Winston Cup Series Circuit and doing business as Signature Racing Photos. She works closely with the NASCAR Public Relations Department and assists them with their objective to increase worldwide exposure of the fastest growing sport in America. Creekmore's photographic work is currently published in several countries around the world.

Matt Dorton has been drawing cartoons for over fifteen years. His feature *Track Laughs* takes a peek at the often humorous side of NASCAR. *Track Laughs* can be seen weekly in *NASCAR Winston Cup Scene* and at *www.tracklaughs.com.* Matt lives near Charlotte, North Carolina, with his wife Kathy and their daughter Abby.

Monte Dutton is in his eleventh year covering NASCAR and is the author of four books on stock-car racing: *At Speed: Up Close and Personal with the People, Places and Fans of NASCAR* (2000); *Jeff Gordon: The Racer* (2000); *Rebel with a Cause: A Season with NASCAR Star Tony Stewart* (2001); and *Postcards from Pit Road: NASCAR's 2002 Season* (2003). He also edited and contributed to *Taking Stock: Life in NASCAR's Fast Lane* (2002). Dutton was the 2000 recipient of the Frank Blunk Memorial Award as the Eastern Motorsports Press Association's writer of the year. A graduate of Furman University, Dutton lives in Clinton, South Carolina.

Carol Einarsson lives in Nebraska and homeschools her eleven-year-old son. She writes three weekly NASCAR columns at *InsiderRacingNews.com* and has hopes of becoming a full-time writer. Contact her at *CheersJeers@aol.com.*

Rob Faiella has been around racing his whole life. He has driven and owned racecars, been a track official and even worked in the past with the 2001–2002 NASCAR Championship Modified Tour Team as a crewmember. He is the publisher and lead writer for *InsideThePitBox.com.* Contact him at *RobFaiella@ InsideThePitBox.com.*

Mike Fields is a lifelong auto-racing fan and drove race cars (briefly) years ago. Mike is on the board of Racing4Kids Children's Charities, writes for *Raceway Media Magazine* (*RacewayMedia.com*), operates *www.LongIslandMotorsports.com* and owns Racers' PR & Motorsports Marketing. He may be reached at *RaceNews@juno.com.*

Norm Froscher is a freelance magazine writer in his fiftieth year of writing, having begun as a newspaper sports writer upon graduation from the University of Florida in 1953. Through the years, Froscher has been honored with the Ray Marquette Memorial Award and the Bloys Britt Memorial Writing Award, and been the winner of annual press competitions. The media center at Gainesville

Raceway is named in his honor. Most recently, he was honored with a Lifetime Achievement Award by the Driver of the Year Foundation and was presented with a Maurice Lecroix Swiss wristwatch. Froscher joins Chris Economaki as the only two racing journalists to be so honored.

Lisa Hancock is a beginning freelance writer who also enjoys photography, travel, horses and outdoor activities. With a full-time job in the auto industry, two daughters and one granddaughter, Lisa is planning on future publications with *Chicken Soup for the Soul*. She and her husband, Jim, live in New Castle, Indiana, and she can be reached at *Ljhancock@peoplepc.com*.

Jonny Hawkins is a full-time freelancer whose cartoons have been published in over fifty books and 265 publications. His two latest books (collaborative works with Bob Phillips), *Heavenly Humor* and *A Tackle Box of Fishing Funnies*, can be found in bookstores or by contacting him at P.O. Box 188, Sherwood, MI 49089 or via e-mail at *jonnyhawkins2nz@yahoo.com*.

Max Helton is founder of Motor Racing Outreach and cofounder/CEO of International Motorsport Services. Both organizations providie a variety of services to the racing communities of the world. He served as chaplain of NASCAR for fourteen years and is the author of numerous books. A sought-after speaker and church consultant, he can be reached at HOPE, P. O. Box 680586, Charlotte, NC 28216 or by calling 704-948-2741. His e-mail address is *maxhelton@aol.com*.

Blair Kerkhoff, his wife Karen and their children, Nate, Ben and Anna, live in Overland Park, Kansas. Blair has been a sportswriter for *The Kansas City Star* since 1989 and previously worked for the *Roanoke Times*. Blair has written four books. He can be reached at *BKerkhoff@kcstar.com*.

Andrew Kossak received a Bachelor of Arts in Communications from Oswego (N.Y.) State in 1992. Andrew is an experienced sports writer, with numerous articles and columns printed in magazines and on Web sites. He and his wife Natalie reside in Maryland. Please contact Andrew at *nak1120@yahoo.com*.

Claire B. Lang is a veteran motorsports journalist and broadcaster. She's heard from coast to coast as an anchor on XM Satellite Radio's NASCAR channel and is a columnist and television feature reporter on *Raceline* seen on affiliates nationwide and on the Outdoor channel. She can be reached at *insiderCBL@aol.com*.

Roy Lang III is an assistant sports editor for *The Times* in Shreveport, Louisiana *(www.shreveporttimes.com)*. He is also the host of a trio of radio shows, two dedicated to auto racing and one to golf. He enjoys playing tournament golf and driving fast. You can reach him at *jrdan23@aol.com*.

John Marshall is a cartoonist living in upstate New York. To check out more of his cartoons, you can view them at *www.Johnmarshallstudios.com*. He is a member of the National Cartoonists Society.

Rick Maynard, a Lexington, Kentucky, native, received his bachelor's degree in journalism from the University of Kentucky in 1989. A freelance artist by night, Rick works by day for NASCAR driver Mark Martin. Rick's NASCAR cartoon, *In the Marbles* (and other cartoons), can be seen at *www. rickmaynard.com.* E-mail Rick at *rick@rickmaynard.com.*

Heather McGee is a licensed mechanic with ten years of experience. She was also a Technical and Pit Official for two years with a Canadian Late Model Stockcar Series. Heather resides in Ontario, Canada. Her interests include horses, her pit bull-cross puppy, reading and, of course, racing.

Matt McLaughlin graduated from Villanova in 1981 summa cum relievo. He's entering his eighth season as a writer for *RacingOne.com.* Hobbies outside of racing involve anything fast and loud with an engine. When not chasing race-cars or old muscle cars, he resides outside of Philadelphia. He can be reached at *Matt@SpeedFX.com.*

Jennifer Meyer is a stay-at-home mom currently working on her master's degree in education and substitute teaching in her spare time. Since writing this story, she found out her cancer has returned and continues to undergo treatment. She resides in north Idaho with her husband, Jeff, and daughter, Grace. She can be reached at *Survivor@povn.com.*

Mark Moore is forty-one years old and has been a NASCAR fan since 1964. He has written about racing for *www.speedwaymedia.com* since September 2001.

Mark Parisi's *Off the Mark* comic panel has been syndicated since 1987 and is distributed by United Media. Mark's humor also graces greeting cards, T-shirts, calendars, magazines (such as *Billboard*), newsletters and books. Lynn is his wife and business partner, and their daughter, Jenny, contributes with inspiration (as do three cats).

David Poole has covered NASCAR for *The Charlotte (N.C.) Observer* and for *www.thatsracin.com* since 1997. A graduate of the University of North Carolina, he has written several racing books, including *Race with Destiny* and *Flat Out and Half Turned Over: Tales from Pit Road with Buddy Baker.* Contact him at *dpoole@charlotteobserver.com.*

Kay Presto has covered motorsports for thirty-two years, receiving fifty-one national and state honors. She has broadcast on ESPN, CNN and all major U.S. radio networks, and done public relations and photojournalism for international books and magazines. She owns Presto Productions, and her bio is in the 2003 *Who's Who of American Women.* E-mail Kay at *prestoprod@juno.com.*

Jennifer Riley received her bachelor of science in journalism from Bowling Green State University in 1996, graduating summa cum laude. She manages the Ford Credit racing sponsorship for Campbell & Co., a marketing commu-nications company based in Dearborn, Michigan. Jennifer lives in the Detroit area with her husband, Kevin, and daughter, Kaitlyn. She can be reached via e-mail at *jenwriting@hotmail.com*.

Barbara Seitz has been published in a *Guideposts* book called *Their Mysterious Ways* and is presently writing her memoir titled *One Last Time*. Barbara was formerly in the antique business and, when not writing, enjoys antiquing, tag sales and reading. She can be reached at *BSeitz8798@aol.com*. Fax her at 860-646-1758.

Mike Shapiro's cartoons have appeared in many publications, including *Barron's, The Wall Street Journal* and the *Harvard Business Review*. His Web site can be found at *www.reuben.org/mikeshapiro*. Mike can be reached by e-mail at *mikeshapiro@mndspring.com*.

Susan Siersma's writing, inspired by everyday life, is dedicated to her close friends and family. Her stories have been published in *Chicken Soup for the Romantic Soul, Inside Line* magazine and *A Cup of Comfort for Mothers and Daughters*. She welcomes correspondence at *ssiersma@msn.com*.

Marty Smith received his bachelor of science degree in media studies from Radford University (Va.) in 1998, where he was named Honors Scholar of the journalism department. Smith is senior writer for *NASCAR.com*, for whom he reports on the top three levels of NASCAR racing. He resides in Huntersville, North Carolina, with his wife, Lainie, and can be reached at *marty.smith@ turner.com* or *MartDawgSmith@aol.com*.

Mike Smith, in addition to his powerful political cartoons, steers his irreverent humor toward the National Association for Stock Car Auto Racing (NASCAR). Smith's weekly Stockcar/Toons™ are distributed by United Features Syndicate to newspapers nationwide, including the *Chicago Sun-Times, Detroit News, Portland Oregonian* and *Washington Times*.

Wayne Spodnick resides in Connecticut and has extensive sports radio expertise with the PGA Tour, NBA and the NHL. He has also written articles for *GOAL Magazine*, the official magazine of the NHL. Wayne is a well-traveled NASCAR fan and amateur photographer. Currently employed in the building products industry, he can be reached at *ctcowboy@aol.com* or 203-770-6990.

Jenni Thompson is a senior at Arkansas State University and will receive her bachelor of science in marketing in May 2003. Jenni's hobbies include watching racing, reading and listening to Elvis Presley music. Her aspirations are to someday work in NASCAR and write her own novel. You can reach Jenni at *jeffgordonfan99@hotmail.com*.

Lori Tyler is a lifelong fan who has spent the last four years serving as assistant editor with *Catchfence.com*. She is also involved with STB Marketing Group, providing public-relations work for the racing public. Ms. Tyler can be reached at *LTyler@catchfence.com*.

Michael Waltrip is one of NASCAR's most popular drivers. While driving the #15 NAPA Chevrolet for Dale Earnhardt, Inc., Michael won the 2001 Daytona 500 for his first NASCAR Winston Cup career victory and followed up in 2002 by winning the Pepsi 400 and the Gatorade Twin-125 qualifying race. Michael resides in Sherrills Ford, North Carolina, with his wife and two children, and lists his hobbies as playing basketball and golf.

Deb Williams is the editor of *NASCAR Winston Cup Scene,* and the only woman to win the top three motorsports journalism awards: National Motorsports Press Association Writer of the Year (twice), Russ Catlin (twice) and Henry T. McLemore. She received her Bachelor of Science, with honors, in journalism with a minor in criminal justice from East Tennessee State University. Deb also has appeared in several NASCAR Winston Cup shows on the Speed Channel. She has written a book on NASCAR team owner and former championship crew chief Ray Evernham and has plans for several others.

Steve Wingate, a 1991 graduate of the University of Alabama at Birmingham, lives in Jasper, Alabama, with his wife and two children. He is the author of over sixty articles on a variety of subjects and creator of the popular Web site "The Car Guy of Benchfield." E-mail Steve at *stevewingate@hotmail.com.*

Brad Winters is the racing editor for *www.sportspedia.com.* He writes the syndicated newspaper columns, "The Athlete's Inspiration," "Racing Inspirations" and "Ask an Andretti." Brad and his wife Diane are the parents of six children and reside in Columbus, Indiana. You can contact Brad at *bradwinters@ sportspedia.com* or 812-371-2714. His address is 4342 River Road, Columbus, IN 47203.

Dennis Yohnka earned his journalism degree at Northern Illinois University. He works full-time for Joliet Township High School, but always makes time for weekend race coverage. His son, Bill, is ready to take over weekly writing responsibilities while Dennis focuses on a dirt-track racing movie script. Contact Dennis at *dyracing@attbi.com.*

Lynne Zielinski lives and writes in Huntsville, Alabama. She believes life is a gift from God and what we do with it is our gift to God. Lynne can be reached via e-mail at *ARISWAY@aol.com.*